Magnolia Table

Magnolia Table

— *a collection of recipes for gathering* —

JOANNA GAINES

WITH MARAH STETS

photography by Amy Neunsinger

𝒲𝓂

WILLIAM MORROW

An Imprint of HarperCollins*Publishers*

also by Joanna Gaines

THE MAGNOLIA STORY

HarperCollins books may be purchased for educational, business, or sales promotional use. For information, please email the Special Markets Department at SPsales@harpercollins.com.

FIRST EDITION

Illustrations © 2017 Andre Junget

Library of Congress Cataloging-in-Publication Data has been applied for.

ISBN 978-0-06-282015-0
ISBN 978-0-06-286216-7 (B&N signed edition)
ISBN 978-0-06-286342-3 (BAM signed edition)
ISBN 978-0-06-286343-0 (Costco signed edition)
ISBN 978-0-06-286198-6 (Target exclusive edition)
ISBN 978-0-06-286199-3 (Target exclusive signed edition)
ISBN 978-0-06-286200-6 (Walmart signed edition)

22   LSC   24

To Chip and the kids,

*You inspire me not only in the kitchen,
but in every part of life. I love to cook,
in no small part, because of the excitement
and appreciation you have shown for my
home-cooked meals all along the way.
Our time together in the kitchen and the
countless hours we have spent around the
table are my favorite memories of all.*

Contents

INTRODUCTION

I like to compare our first month of marriage to free-falling through the air with no idea how or where we would land. Chip and I had just started renovating a really small house that I couldn't wait to call home, while also renovating my little shop on Bosque. If you're familiar with our story, then you may remember that we bought the building on Bosque because Chip had encouraged me to start my own business after I'd quietly dreamed about it for years. Before then, I had never really taken any true risks. I didn't like trying things that I might not be good at because I believed that failure was a bad thing, and therefore, not an option. Looking back, there's no telling what I missed out on because I was too scared to try something new or because I gave up on something that may have been a little uncomfortable before I could see the reward in it. I preferred feeling safe to being stretched. But after only a month of marriage, Chip was already somehow making risk look fun. He sincerely believed that failure could be a valuable thing, and I was beginning to see that it didn't need to be something I feared. Chip was teaching me that even if I failed at something, I could just get back up and try again.

We were newlyweds and uncertain about how to do this thing called marriage. As we got closer to finishing the updates on the house, I had two looming thoughts in the back of my mind: "How do I even begin to decorate a house?" and "What in the world am I going to cook in our new kitchen?" I was feeling way out of my comfort zone as a new wife and putting a ton of pressure on myself. But I was determined to put my best foot forward and try my hand in the kitchen. My sister-in-law, Shannon, had given me one of the best wedding presents: a cookbook full of Gaines family recipes. To be honest, at the time I was mostly just intimidated by the thought of cooking full meals, but it still meant so much and made me feel truly welcomed into their family.

As we got close to spending our first night in the renovated house, I started combing through the recipes Shannon had shared with me, looking for inspiration. They sounded delicious, but really unfamiliar. Since I wasn't one to try something new and was terrified of ruining a beloved family recipe, I decided that the very first thing I'd serve Chip was *my* mom's spaghetti. It was one of my favorites, and it was really simple to make. She browned ground beef in a skillet and added a jar of store-bought marinara sauce while she boiled thin noodles. Mom would mix it all together in a bowl after it was cooked and serve it with warm bread and butter on the side. This meal embodied comfort and safety to me. It felt like home. To this day, whenever I eat spaghetti, that warm, fuzzy feeling hits me and I feel like all is right in the world.

That evening, I set the table with our new dishes, lit a few candles, served water in nice wineglasses (we were on a tight budget, but the glasses made the water seem fancy), and dished out the spaghetti for Chip. I was feeling pretty confident that this was a fail-safe meal to serve to my new husband in our new home. He took two bites and didn't say anything. That was probably the first time since we'd met that he'd been at a loss for words. I figured he was just in awe of what was in front of him and trying to process how much he loved it. After six bites I couldn't handle the silence so I asked him what he thought.

And then he said these words: "Welllll, umm, it doesn't taste like my mom's spaghetti."

I almost choked on my noodles. A few not-so-nice thoughts (and words) were running through my mind, but I kept quiet and let him continue to dig himself even deeper into this hole.

"I just love my mom's spaghetti. I wish you would have asked her for her recipe. This tastes different, and I'm just used to my mom's."

I got up from the table, cleared away his plate, and told him he could do the dishes and clean up the mess in the kitchen. I was *done*. Let's just say he learned his lesson. But I learned a valuable one that night as well. Food is *personal*. It's like the musical soundtrack of our lives, and it can take us back to a particular moment in time—good or bad. Food is also emotional. It connects us to our past. Chip's deep loyalty to his mom's spaghetti is actually really sweet. I love and appreciate it now, fifteen years later. And back then, I eventually realized that we were both just missing our mamas and anxious about adjusting to this new, unfamiliar chapter of life. Food was the symbol of everything we'd known up until then. And through my cooking that meal and Chip's reaction to it, we were in fact communicating everything we were experiencing in that moment, as newlyweds at our own table, in our own home.

It wasn't until I was pregnant with our first son, Drake, that I started to step it up in the kitchen. This happened mainly because I was having the oddest cravings. Many times I would want something so particular that I had no choice but to whip it up myself. I don't think I ever made anything too amazing; I just know that I tried. Chip also knew by then to encourage me in my efforts—or else he'd have to go get takeout.

There are two things I remember distinctly about those early days in our marriage. One, I really loved the act of putting on an apron. I think it was because it felt nostalgic and also because it reminded me of my grandmother. And, two, I had a domed glass cake stand on our counter that I never liked to see empty. There was something about having it filled up that made the kitchen feel right to me. I always had fresh cookie dough in the fridge so I could quickly bake a batch of cookies or I'd make a quick Bundt cake to put on that stand.

It was in that season that I learned how to prepare a lot of the meals from the book of family recipes that my sister-in-law had given me, like the Gaines chili and a favorite breakfast: warm Malt-o-Meal served with butter and brown sugar and a side of toast for dipping. Chip also tried some of my family's favorites, like my mom's bulgogi (Korean marinated beef) and the Stevens family breakfast tradition: toasted peanut butter and jelly sandwiches dipped in black coffee. Apparently both families liked to dip, a tradition all of our children happily carry on.

Fast-forward to life with three more kids, and by then even an occasional meal at a restaurant wasn't really an option anymore. Our first four children are pretty close in age, and when Emmie Kay was born, we had four kids aged four and under. We quickly realized that it was just easier to feed them at home rather than in public. That season of my life wasn't about making the most beautiful meals. It was just about *making* a meal that would nourish my growing family. I really appreciated cookbooks that made things easy for a busy mom. Simple ingredients, minimal prep time, and really yummy dishes for young and adult palates alike. Casseroles, Crock-Pot dinners, and big pots of hearty soup that could simmer for a while became my go-to meals. Even today, these are my favorite choices when we have a busy week.

Then, as our kids got older and could better articulate their preferences, I began to really enjoy cooking for them. I loved hearing what they liked and what they were craving. There's nothing sweeter to me than the time we spend around the table. The moments shared over a meal are well worth the preparation and the work that go into making it. Food has come to play such an integral role in our family that the meaning of "seasonality" has expanded beyond just what's growing in the garden. It's also about what's happening in our lives. When I plan the meals for the week, I really take into account each of our individual schedules. It's important to acknowledge the season of life we're in as well as the season unfolding outside and make practical food decisions to support both. When it's a quiet week, each kid gets to pick the menu for a night. They would much rather eat a warm meal at home than go to a restaurant in town. The kids seem to be growing up quicker than ever, and a home-cooked meal is the thing that connects us all the most. When Drake went to summer camp for the first time this past year, he mailed me quite a few letters that said things like "Dear Mom, when I get home, can you please make me a lemon pie?? And also fatayar?" There was something about the thought of his mama's cooking that consoled and was a comfort to Drake when he was missing home.

Life is busier these days and honestly it can be harder to find the time to cook meals from scratch, but it's important enough to me to prioritize it. Cooking has become something that's not only good for my family but for me, too. When I'm at work, I'm making so many business and creative decisions that my mind gets into a mode that's legitimately hard to turn off when I get home. I find it difficult to be fully present when I am still processing all that happened during the day.

But then . . .

I stick my hand in a bowl of flour to begin to make a pie crust, or peel some potatoes, and all of a sudden my thoughts slow down. I begin to unwind. I turn on my favorite music, open the kitchen window, and let the background noise of the kids playing with Chip set my mind at ease. These are the sounds that signal to my heart and my mind that I am home.

The kitchen actually reminds me a lot of the garden. You put your hands to work and tend to it, and when the harvest comes, it gives back to you a hundredfold. There is a reward that comes from working with your hands, whether it's in your home, garden, or kitchen. We can choose to view the everyday tasks of life as either chores or gifts. It's powerful how just a slight change in perspective can transform something that you dread into something you look forward to. For me, this whole cooking thing has become one of the things I look forward to most and I wouldn't trade my time in the kitchen for anything.

This cookbook is a celebration of bringing people together. I share many of my favorite personal recipes as well as some from friends and family, and of course from our restaurant, Magnolia Table. You'll see in every recipe that I've included prep, cook, and cool times. These are estimates, so please don't take them too literally. This is just how it works for me when I'm cooking for my family. A recipe that takes me 30 minutes to prepare might take you half or twice the time. Just as some people chop faster than others, some ovens heat quicker as well. If the recipe takes you longer or doesn't look like the photograph, please don't be hard on yourself. A huge part of cooking is owning and enjoying the experience. Similar to my design philosophy about making your space uniquely yours, I want you to feel inspired to personalize these recipes and adjust them as you need for your family's tastes. If you don't like onions, take them out! If you love mushrooms, add more! Just because a recipe is in the breakfast chapter doesn't mean that you have to serve it for breakfast. In fact, I encourage you to switch it up more often than not. There are no gospel truths on these pages. I'm not a professional chef. I'm just a busy, working mama who loves to cook and share recipes.

And I'm not trying to achieve perfection in the kitchen. If I were, I'd be exhausted by the time we all got around the table to enjoy it—and that would really defeat the purpose. That's why you'll see things within these pages that might look like contradictions, but are truly the ways I cook for my family. For example, I often buy organic meat and I grow lots of the vegetables we eat, but I consider store-bought refrigerated dough and boxed broth to be gifts from the heavens. I love to make pie crust from scratch when I have time, but I always have store-bought on hand so I can whip up a quick quiche. I keep my pantry stocked with all the ingredients I need to make pancakes from scratch, but oftentimes I make them from a mix or heat up frozen waffles when the mornings are just too busy for anything else. And if I don't have time to bake a fresh pie for dessert, I buy one at the store and make fresh whipped cream for the topping.

Whether you picked up this book because you want to try your hand in the kitchen for the first time or because you want to add a few new dishes to the collection of meals you have been serving for years, my hope is that you are inspired beyond the food and the photography to discover ways to make meals that are uniquely yours. No matter what happens, try to enjoy the process. As Chip told me early on: If you mess up, there's always pizza.

Joanna

The Pantry

Here's what I always have on hand in my fridge and pantry for when I want to whip up something quick, whether it's dinner or freshly baked cookies.

REFRIGERATED

- ☐ Salted butter
- ☐ Buttermilk
- ☐ Half-and-half
- ☐ Heavy (whipping) cream
- ☐ 2% organic milk
- ☐ Sour cream
- ☐ Cream cheese
- ☐ Eggs (see Note)

PRODUCE

- ☐ Bananas
- ☐ Lemons
- ☐ White onions
- ☐ Fresh garlic and jarred chopped garlic

DRY GOODS

- ☐ Unbleached all-purpose flour
- ☐ Self-rising flour
- ☐ Baking powder
- ☐ Baking soda
- ☐ Active dry yeast

- ☐ Refrigerated pie crust
- ☐ Pancake mix
- ☐ Light brown sugar
- ☐ Powdered sugar
- ☐ Granulated sugar
- ☐ Natural unsweetened cocoa powder
- ☐ Semisweet chocolate chips
- ☐ Pecans
- ☐ Ground cinnamon
- ☐ Pure vanilla extract
- ☐ Canned cream of chicken soup
- ☐ Boxed organic chicken broth
- ☐ Assorted types of dry pasta: I usually have a couple of boxes of long pasta, such as fettuccine or spaghetti, and a couple of boxes of short pasta such as farfalle (bow ties).
- ☐ Dark chocolate–covered almonds: These aren't for cooking but for my sanity!

SPICES

- ☐ Kosher salt
- ☐ Parsley flakes
- ☐ Garlic salt
- ☐ Garlic powder
- ☐ Black pepper: I usually buy whole black peppercorns in bottles that have a grinder attached. Black pepper is so much better when freshly ground, and I love the convenience of these.

OILS

- ☐ Extra virgin olive oil: For cooking and vinaigrettes
- ☐ Vegetable oil: I usually have canola oil on hand. Whatever neutral oil you like will work fine.
- ☐ Vegetable oil spray and nonstick baking spray with flour

NOTE: *In the United States it is commonly believed that eggs need to be kept in the fridge, which is the case when you buy them refrigerated from the store. We leave ours out on the counter because they are coming straight from the coop and have not previously been chilled.*

Tools

When Chip and I were first married, our kitchen drawers didn't have much more than a couple of knives, a vegetable peeler, and a can opener, and we did just fine for a while. After cooking for a few years, I learned that while there is certainly no need for a lot of fancy equipment to make amazing food, a few trusted tools can make it easier and more enjoyable. These are the tools I use most often.

GLASS MEASURING CUPS

With graduated lines to measure hot and cold liquid ingredients, these are an everyday essential. I use them for everything, from beating an egg before brushing it on biscuits to melting chocolate in the microwave. I have several ranging in size from 1 cup to 8 cups, and I prefer Pyrex because they're sturdy and dishwasher safe.

MEASURING CUPS

I use my pretty wood-handled sets for light jobs, but when I'm really cooking up a storm, I need sturdy, dishwasher-safe cups that come in a wide variety of sizes. At a minimum, most sets include ¼, ⅓, ½, and 1 cup. For convenience it's good to have a few more sizes, such as ⅔ and ¾ cup, and even ⅛ cup, which is the equivalent of 2 tablespoons. Cups with the measurements embossed rather than printed are ideal because the marks won't fade.

MEASURING SPOONS

Just as with measuring cups, I like dishwasher-safe spoons in a lot of different sizes, with the measurements embossed. The standard four-piece set usually has ¼ teaspoon, ½ teaspoon, 1 teaspoon, and 1 tablespoon. It's very helpful to have ⅛ teaspoon and ¾ teaspoon, as well as ½ tablespoon, which is the equivalent of 1½ teaspoons.

BISCUIT CUTTERS

These are like a perfectly round cookie cutter but with higher sides and a sturdy handle on top. Often sold in sets of three or more in varying sizes. Good cutters have a sharp edge to cut cleanly through biscuit dough.

WOODEN SPOONS

These are inexpensive, heat resistant, useful for cooking all kinds of dishes, and easy to clean by hand.

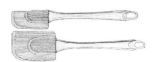

RUBBER OR SILICONE SPATULAS

These flexible scrapers and stirrers are indispensable. I like to have a large size and one that's a bit smaller. If you're using a spatula only for stirring and scraping cold or room-temperature ingredients, choose a head made from either rubber or silicone, but only silicone should be used in hot pans; rubber can melt at high temperatures. I like dishwasher-safe spatulas, so I tend to avoid wooden handles, which can dry out after repeated rinse cycles.

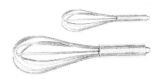

WHISKS

I have two whisks, one large and one small, that I use for blending and whipping ingredients.

SLOTTED SPOON

A large spoon with several slots is ideal for stirring pasta and draining the liquid from solid ingredients, like when I transfer my pickled jalapeños from the hot brine into individual jars.

METAL SPATULA

We eat a lot of pancakes and grilled cheese sandwiches in our house, and a good sturdy metal spatula is invaluable to get the job done right.

LADLE

I make soups and stews often, and a quality ladle is the only way to serve them. I find a long-handled ladle is most useful so that I can serve from tall stockpots as well as shorter saucepans.

HINGED CITRUS PRESS

I love lemon juice and I end up adding it to many dishes. If I need the juice from just one or two lemon halves, I'll often squeeze them with my hands, but any more than that and I reach for my hinged citrus press. It does a great job of getting every last bit of juice out of each half and it helpfully strains out the seeds.

CHEF'S KNIFE

No kitchen tools are more important than good knives, and I think a chef's knife in particular is one of the few things that's worth spending whatever you can afford. A well-made knife that holds a sharp blade will last years and will certainly prove itself to be worth every penny. I have a knife with an 8-inch blade for chopping and slicing all kinds of ingredients.

PARING KNIFE

This small knife with a slightly curved blade fits neatly in the hand. I probably use my paring knife every day for so many different things: slicing apples, peeling onions, halving lemons, topping and tailing green beans, trimming vegetables, and chopping small amounts of garlic or onion.

BIRD'S BEAK KNIFE

This type of paring knife has a distinct concave blade and a thin, sharp tip. I use it most of the same ways I use a paring knife, but not for chopping on a cutting board.

VEGETABLE PEELER

I use my sturdy peeler not only for the obvious—peeling vegetables and fruit—but also for cutting items such as asparagus and carrots into long, thin strips and shaving cheese or chocolate.

MICROPLANE GRATER

This handheld grater with a long rasp is a great tool for grating citrus zest or fresh garlic.

MARBLE ROLLING PIN

I love a beautiful, wooden rolling pin to place on a shelf or counter, but for everyday cooking I'll reach for my marble rolling pin. It stays cold, which is important when rolling buttery pastry, and it's heavy so it doesn't take too much effort to roll dough very thin when that's what the recipe requires.

TONGS

I have a few pairs of tongs in different lengths, with both metal and silicone pincers, and I use them for tossing pasta or salad, sautéing chicken cutlets, flipping tenderloins on the grill, and lots of other tasks. Choose strong tongs with comfortable handles, and they're easier to store if they can be locked in the closed position.

BOX GRATER

A sturdy four-sided box grater with different-sized grating holes on each side makes it easy to grate cheese and hearty vegetables and fruit.

IMMERSION BLENDER

Making velvety smooth soups and sauces is so easy with a handheld immersion or stick blender because I don't have to fuss with transferring piping-hot ingredients to a blender.

PASTRY BLENDER

This U-shaped tool has several curved metal wires and a handle. It is used to mix solid fat such as butter or shortening into flour to make pastry dough like pie crusts, biscuits, or scones.

EXTRA-LARGE STAINLESS-STEEL BOWL

The biggest bowl in most mixing bowl sets isn't large enough to hold the amounts of dough I need to make big batches of cinnamon squares or biscuits. That's when I pull out my extra-large, 16-quart bowl, which is also great for preparing salad for a crowd. Before you buy one, confirm the measurements of both the bowl and the cabinet or shelf on which you'll store it so you can be sure it will fit.

NESTING STAINLESS-STEEL MIXING BOWLS

Every home cook needs mixing bowls in a variety of sizes, and I highly recommend buying a matching set that can be stacked for convenient storage. Choose bowls that are light but not flimsy and have sturdy, flat bottoms so they don't wobble.

SMALL PREP BOWLS AND RAMEKINS

When I'm cooking, I use 2-ounce, stackable prep bowls and 4- to 8-ounce ramekins to hold all the little things that are prepped or measured along the way, such as spices, minced garlic, chopped herbs, and lemon juice.

PIE PLATES

I make a lot of quiches and pies and have an ever-growing collection of assorted pie plates. My favorite ones are weighty (flimsy pans lead to burned crust) and made of stoneware, clay, or ceramic.

BAKING SHEETS

I bake cookies on my heavy-duty, rimmed, aluminum, 18 x 13-inch baking sheets, but that's far from the only thing I use them for. I also roast vegetables and meat on them, and I slide them under pies while they bake to protect the oven floor from potential drips. I also use them to hold trimmed vegetables prepped for grilling or roasting. Honestly, there are very few meals I make where at least one baking sheet isn't called into service in one way or another.

LARGE CAST-IRON SKILLET

A 10- to 12-inch cast-iron skillet is an inexpensive, durable stovetop and oven-safe pan to use for everything from frying donuts, to cooking bacon, to baking cornbread and frittatas. Once the pan is well seasoned (you can buy them this way or do it yourself following the directions that come with the pan), it's essentially a nonstick pan with an almost indestructible surface. The best way to keep cast iron in good shape is to wash it by hand under running water, using little to no soap, and blot it dry with a towel. Use a paper towel to rub vegetable oil on the inside of the pan until it is well coated but there is no excess oil. Heat the pan on the stovetop or in the oven until it is completely dry.

TALL STOCKPOT

We are a family who loves leftovers. I often make big batches of family favorites like chicken and dumplings or chili in a very tall stockpot. I love it because it holds a ton without taking up a lot of excess space on the stovetop.

DEEP CASSEROLE DISH

A standard 9 x 13-inch pan with 2-inch-high sides works perfectly for most casseroles. Some of my family's favorites, like chicken pot pie, have really big yields, and for these I use a 9 x 13-inch pan with 3-inch-high sides because of its larger capacity.

PARCHMENT PAPER AND WAX PAPER

These two papers make cleaning up after baking and roasting so much easier, but they are not interchangeable. Wax paper should never be directly exposed to the heat of the oven, so it's used to line pans that are completely filled with batter to make it easier to allow baked cakes and breads to come out of the pan easily. Parchment paper can be exposed to the oven's heat. It's used to line baking pans to create a grease-free nonstick surface for baking cookies and roasting vegetables. It can also be folded into airtight packages to cook fish in the oven.

CUTTING BOARDS

I have a whole bunch of white dishwasher-safe cutting boards in all different sizes. I prefer boards that have a thin groove around the outer edge to catch liquid so it doesn't spill all over the counter.

MORTAR AND PESTLE

Putting spices in a heavy mortar and crushing them with a pestle gives you control over how fine or coarse the spices are ground. I use my mortar and pestle primarily for crushing the anise seed for Syrian donuts and black peppercorns for salads.

FOOD PROCESSOR

I use my food processor at least once a week to make fresh salsa, mix the dough for drop biscuits, or blend the filling for cinnamon squares. I use it so often and for such large quantities that I finally splurged for a bigger-than-average food processor a few years ago. I love that I can process everything in a single batch.

ELECTRIC STAND MIXER

A heavy-duty freestanding mixer is helpful for anyone who loves to bake as much as I do. The best part of it might not even be how well it does its mixing, beating, and whipping jobs. I think it's that you can walk away while it does the work for you. Just be careful not to walk too far away from something that needs watching, like egg whites or cream.

HANDHELD ELECTRIC MIXER

I love my stand mixer for all the big jobs, but when I need to mix up a smaller batch of something, I prefer to use my handheld electric mixer and a stainless-steel bowl.

CHAPTER 1

Breakfast

BREAKFAST

Chip *loves* breakfast. It's absolutely his favorite meal. He firmly believes that starting our family off with a warm meal in our bellies is the best way to set everyone up for a great day. He's so enthusiastic about it that for years he has dreamed of opening up a restaurant that's all about breakfast. It was especially thrilling to be a part of making his dream come true when we opened Magnolia Table in Waco, where the heart and soul of the menu is breakfast, served all day long.

Like his passion for so many things, Chip's enthusiasm for breakfast is contagious. Thanks to him, our kids get to look forward to a hot breakfast nearly every morning, and I've come to appreciate how grounding it is for all of us to spend a little time together in the morning over a warm, nourishing meal. The challenge, of course, is finding the time for it—not only to prepare something for everyone but also to get all of us to the table at once on a busy morning. Half the time Chip prepares it and the other half I do, and as the kids get older they've started to help out a little more, too. The boys like to make scrambled eggs and they've gotten really good at it. Believe me, there are certainly times when I pop some frozen waffles in the toaster, add lots of softened butter and warm maple syrup, and call it good. (A hot breakfast is a hot breakfast . . . right, Chip?)

But most often we do something more substantial, and we've discovered some great tricks to make this possible. Just after the kids go to bed, I'll spend fifteen minutes assembling a quick casserole, like overnight French toast or Eggs Benedict casserole, and refrigerate it so that Chip can put it in the oven first thing in the morning. Sometimes I'll mix up the liquid and dry ingredients separately for ricotta pancakes so the next morning they can be stirred together quickly and poured onto the griddle—and it takes only a few minutes.

There's a reason I call breakfast Chip's love language, and it's not simply that he loves to eat it. It's because of what all of us sitting around the table together and sharing a hot breakfast means to him. It's about taking the time to pause before we all head out into the world. And I think there's no lovelier way to start the day.

JOJO'S BISCUITS

It took me a year of Saturdays to get these biscuits just right. Almost every weekend for months I worked up another batch for Chip and the kids to taste and then wrote down their feedback. Biscuit after biscuit was judged to be too heavy, too light, too flat, too salty, too dry, or just . . . not right. I don't entirely know what kept me going back to the mixing bowl, but something inside me was clearly determined to prevail. All those failed batches didn't discourage me—instead each one spurred me to tweak my formula and try again the next week. Of course it helped that I had a houseful of agreeable taste testers who delivered their criticisms with kindness, and encouraged me to keep at it with the kind of enthusiasm that can only be mustered by people who really *love biscuits.*

I vividly remember the moment I finally nailed it, when the whole family declared simultaneously, "This is it." *They have been our family's Saturday-morning breakfast ever since. Among the tricks I worked out along the way are the somewhat unusual addition of eggs and the way they are arranged for baking so that they all touch, both of which contribute to the moisture, lightness, and loft of these biscuits.*

Chip thinks they are nothing less than heaven on earth. Every Saturday he has the same breakfast—fried eggs cooked over-medium and two biscuits, one slathered with butter and strawberry jam and the other one tucked under a generous serving of sausage gravy. Every week he declares that it's the best breakfast he has ever had. And every week the kids reply, "Dad, you say that every time!" *These biscuits have become so ingrained in our lives that when our oldest, Drake, went away to summer camp for the first time he wrote me a card that said, in part, "Dear Mom, I miss you so much. All I can think about is home and your biscuits and gravy. Promise me that as soon I get back, we'll have biscuits and gravy." Naturally, I framed the card.*

When we opened Magnolia Table, there was no question these biscuits had to be on the menu, so I turned the recipe over to the chefs to transform it to suit the needs of a restaurant kitchen. (I make only twenty at a time; they make hundreds of them every day.) When the time came to decide which of my family's favorites would go in this cookbook, I knew not only that I had to share the biscuits, but also that the recipe had to be the very first one in the book.

JOJO'S BISCUITS

PREP: 20 minutes, plus at least 30 minutes chilling	**COOK**: 15 to 20 minutes	**COOL**: 5 minutes

4 cups self-rising flour, plus more for the work surface

2 tablespoons baking powder

1 teaspoon baking soda

¾ pound (3 sticks) salted butter, cold, cut into ½-inch pieces or grated

2 large eggs, beaten, plus 1 large egg for brushing

1½ cups buttermilk, or as needed, plus 1 tablespoon for brushing

Pop's Strawberry Jam or Bobo's Classic Gravy, for serving (optional; pages 20–21)

1. In a large bowl, whisk together the flour, baking powder, and baking soda. Add the butter and use a pastry blender to cut the butter into the flour until the pieces are even and about the size of peas. (See photo a.)

2. Stir in the beaten eggs with a wooden spoon until combined. Stir in 1½ cups buttermilk until the dough comes together into a sticky mass. If it is too dry, add more buttermilk 1 tablespoon at a time, mixing after each addition, until it reaches the correct consistency. Cover the bowl and refrigerate for at least 30 minutes and up to overnight.

3. Position a rack in the middle of the oven and preheat the oven to 400°F. Line a baking sheet with parchment paper.

4. Scrape the dough onto a floured work surface. Use your floured hands to press it into a round roughly 14 inches across and about ½ inch thick.

5. Use a floured 2¾-inch round cutter to cut out about 20 biscuits. If necessary, collect and pat out the scraps to cut more biscuits. (See photo b.)

6. Transfer the biscuits to the prepared baking sheet, arranging them so that they all are touching.

7. In a small dish, beat together the remaining egg and 1 tablespoon buttermilk. Brush the mixture on the top of the biscuits. (See photo c.)

8. Bake until golden brown, 15 to 20 minutes. Let cool slightly in the pan on a rack. (See photo d.)

9. Biscuits are best the day they are made (and ideally fresh out of the oven!). Serve with strawberry jam or gravy, if desired. Store leftovers in an airtight container at room temperature for up to 2 days.

Makes about 20 biscuits

NOTE: *For longer storage, arrange the unbaked biscuits about ½ inch apart on two parchment-paper-lined baking sheets and freeze until solid. Transfer them to a zip-top plastic bag and freeze for up to 2 weeks. There is no need to thaw them before baking.*

a

b

c

d

POP'S STRAWBERRY JAM

To me there's nothing better on a biscuit than a sweet jam, and our family friend Pop's recipe is one of my favorites. It reminds me of breakfasts I had when I was a kid.

PREP: *15 minutes*	COOK: *10 minutes, plus 20 minutes for processing the jars*	COOL: *24 hours*

5 cups (2½ pints) strawberries, rinsed and hulled

One 1.75-ounce packet powdered pectin

7 cups sugar

1 tablespoon salted butter

1. Have ready 8 clean ½-pint (8-ounce) canning jars, canning lids, and rings.

2. Place the empty jars right side up on a rack in a boiling water canner. Fill the canner with water to cover the jars by 1 inch. Bring to a simmer. Keep the jars in the hot water until needed. Wash the lids and rings in warm, soapy water and rinse thoroughly. Set aside to dry.

3. In a food processor, process the strawberries until the desired consistency is reached: For chunkier jelly leave more clumps, or blend well for a smooth texture. Transfer the strawberries to a large saucepan and add the pectin. Bring to a boil over medium-high heat. Stir in the sugar and butter. Bring to a rolling boil and cook for 1 minute. Immediately remove the pan from the heat.

4. Use a jar lifter to remove the jars from the canner, carefully pouring the water inside each jar back into the canner. Pour the hot jam into the jars, filling each jar to ½ inch from the top rim (a jar funnel makes it easy to do this without spilling the hot mixture).

5. Carefully wipe the rims and sides of each jar. Place the lids on top and screw the rings on, tightening them by hand.

6. Place the filled jars on the rack in the water canner. Make sure the water in the canner covers the jars by 1 to 2 inches. Cover the canner and bring the water to a rolling boil. Boil for 10 minutes. Turn off the heat and uncover the canner. Let stand for 5 minutes.

7. Use a jar lifter to carefully remove the jars and place on a towel on the counter. Let the jars stand without moving them for 24 hours.

8. Check the jars to make sure they are properly sealed: Press on the center of each lid; it should not flex. Unscrew each ring and try to lift the lids with your fingers. If they can't be lifted, the seal is good. Screw the rings back on, label the jars, and store in a dark, cool place for up to 6 months. (If the center of a lid flexes when pressed or the lid can be removed, refrigerate that jar and use within 1 week.)

9. Once opened, refrigerate jars of jam for up to 2 weeks.

Makes eight ½-pint jars

BOBO'S CLASSIC GRAVY

Chip's dad, Bob (the kids call him Bobo), makes the best sausage gravy I've ever tasted. And biscuits for breakfast wouldn't be the same without a serving of this rich gravy on top. The yield here is generous because we often have neighbors over for breakfast on Saturday morning and I always want to be sure I have enough to go around. You can easily cut the recipe in half if you prefer, but consider yourself warned: This gravy goes fast. In the unlikely event that you have lots of leftovers, you can keep it in the fridge for a few days and it reheats beautifully.

PREP: *5 minutes*	COOK: *25 minutes*	COOL: *none*

Two 12-ounce packages pork sausage patties, preferably Jimmy Dean

⅓ to ½ cup all-purpose flour, or as needed

4 cups milk, or as needed

Kosher salt and freshly ground black pepper

1. In a large skillet, cook the sausage patties over medium heat until cooked through and nicely browned on both sides, about 15 to 20 minutes, flipping them halfway through cooking. (Do this in batches if necessary.) Transfer the sausage to a platter and set aside.

2. Whisk ⅓ cup flour into the rendered grease in the skillet. Whisk in the milk until smooth. Bring to a simmer over medium heat and cook until slightly thickened, about 5 minutes. Adjust the gravy's consistency if necessary: If it is too thin, whisk in more flour 1 tablespoon at a time, or if it is too thick, add milk a couple tablespoons at a time.

3. Chop the reserved sausage and stir it into the gravy. Season generously with salt and pepper. Serve warm.

4. Store leftovers in a covered container in the refrigerator for up to 4 days. Reheat gently over low heat.

Makes about 6 cups; 10 servings

MUSHROOM, SPINACH & SWISS CHEESE QUICHE

One of the great things about living on a farm is that we always have a surplus of fresh eggs in the barn. Gathering these colorful beauties never gets old. Our family eats fresh eggs at almost every breakfast, so I've got to change things up for them every now and then. Quiche is simple to make and tastes so good—plus it uses up a lot of eggs—so I have a bunch of great recipes for it. I love its versatility and the fact that it surpasses the sum of its parts. Whether it's served at an elegant brunch or at the breakfast table, a beautiful quiche makes the moment seem a bit more celebratory. Depending on how much time I have, I either make my own pie crust or use a store-bought one.

PREP: *10 minutes*	**COOK**: *1 hour*	**COOL**: *5 to 10 minutes*

2 tablespoons salted butter

⅓ cup finely diced white onion

12 ounces baby bella mushrooms, trimmed and sliced (about 4 cups)

2 cups baby spinach (about 2 ounces)

6 large eggs

1 cup heavy cream

1 teaspoon garlic powder

1 teaspoon kosher salt

1 teaspoon freshly ground black pepper

12 ounces Swiss cheese, grated (about 3 cups)

1 unbaked Pie Crust (page 28), or a store-bought 9-inch pie crust

1. Preheat the oven to 350°F.

2. In a large sauté pan, heat the butter over medium heat until melted. Add the onion and sauté until tender, about 6 minutes. Add the mushrooms and sauté until they have given up their liquid and it has mostly evaporated, 5 to 6 minutes. Add the spinach and sauté until wilted, 1 to 2 minutes. Remove from the heat and set aside.

3. In a large bowl, whisk together the eggs, cream, garlic powder, salt, and pepper. Stir in the spinach/mushroom mixture and the Swiss cheese. Pour the mixture into the unbaked pie shell.

4. Bake until the quiche is lightly golden and set in the center when the pan is gently pushed, about 45 minutes. If the crust is browning too quickly, cover it with foil to prevent it from burning.

5. Remove from the oven and let stand for 5 to 10 minutes before serving. Cut into 6 or 8 slices and serve warm or at room temperature.

6. The quiche is best served the day it is made. Tightly wrap leftovers with plastic wrap and store in the refrigerator for up to 2 days.

Makes 6 to 8 servings

THREE-CHEESE QUICHE

It's hard to find a better way to enjoy two of my favorite ingredients—eggs and cheese—than this creamy quiche. Serve it for breakfast with fruit salad or for lunch with lightly dressed spring greens.

PREP: *15 minutes*	**COOK:** *40 to 45 minutes*	**COOL:** *5 to 10 minutes*

6 large eggs

1 cup heavy cream

1 teaspoon garlic powder

½ teaspoon sweet paprika (optional)

1 teaspoon kosher salt

½ teaspoon ground white pepper

4 ounces extra-sharp white Cheddar cheese, grated (about 1 cup)

1 ounce Parmesan cheese, grated (about ½ cup)

2 ounces Gruyère cheese, grated (about ½ cup)

1 unbaked Pie Crust (page 28), or a store-bought 9-inch pie crust

¼ cup minced chives

1. Preheat the oven to 350°F.

2. In a large bowl, whisk together the eggs, cream, garlic powder, paprika (if using), salt, and white pepper.

3. Stir in the Cheddar, Parmesan, and Gruyère.

4. Pour the mixture into the unbaked pie shell. Sprinkle the chives on top.

5. Bake until the quiche is lightly golden and set in the center when the pan is gently pushed, 40 to 45 minutes. If the crust is browning too quickly, cover it with foil to prevent it from burning.

6. Remove from the oven and let stand for 5 to 10 minutes before serving. Cut into 6 or 8 slices and serve warm or at room temperature.

7. The quiche is best served the day it is made. Tightly wrap leftovers with plastic wrap and store in the refrigerator for up to 2 days.

Makes 6 to 8 servings

ASPARAGUS & FONTINA QUICHE

Mild, buttery Fontina cheese is delightful paired with earthy asparagus, but if you can't find it, you can replace it with provolone, or use all Gruyère here. Sometimes I shave the asparagus into thin strips, though simply chopping it works great when I'm more pressed for time. This quiche is beautiful either way.

PREP: *15 minutes*	**COOK**: *50 to 55 minutes*	**COOL**: *5 to 10 minutes*

1 pound asparagus, ends trimmed

6 large eggs

1 cup heavy cream

1 teaspoon garlic salt

1 teaspoon freshly ground black pepper

8 ounces Fontina cheese, grated (about 2 cups)

2 ounces Gruyère cheese, grated (about ½ cup)

1 unbaked Pie Crust (page 28), or a store-bought 9-inch pie crust

1. Preheat the oven to 350°F.

2. Using a vegetable peeler, slice the asparagus lengthwise into long, thin strips, starting just under the tip of each stalk. Leave the tips whole. (Alternatively, cut the asparagus into 1-inch pieces.)

3. In a pot with a steamer insert or in a covered sauté pan fitted with an expandable steamer basket, bring 2 inches of water to a boil. Add the asparagus to the steamer insert or basket, cover, and steam until tender, about 30 seconds for strips and about 3 minutes for pieces.

4. Rinse the asparagus under cold water to stop the cooking. Drain well and set aside.

5. In a large bowl, whisk together the eggs, cream, garlic salt, and pepper. Stir in the Fontina, Gruyère, and reserved asparagus.

6. Pour the mixture into the unbaked pie shell.

7. Bake until lightly golden and set in the center when the pan is gently pushed, 40 to 45 minutes. If the crust is browning too quickly, cover it with foil to prevent it from burning.

8. Remove from the oven and let stand for 5 to 10 minutes before serving. Cut into 6 or 8 slices and serve warm or at room temperature.

9. The quiche is best served the day it is made. Tightly wrap leftovers with plastic wrap and store in the refrigerator for up to 2 days.

Makes 6 to 8 servings

PIE CRUST

When I have a little extra time to make crust for quiche or pie from scratch, I make this buttery one. It can be used for savory and sweet pies and it freezes well. You can even make a double batch and freeze one disk so that all you have to do the next time is roll it out.

PREP: *20 minutes,* *plus 2 hours chilling*	COOK: *under 25 minutes,* *if blind baking*	COOL: *as directed* *in the pie recipe*

1¼ cups all-purpose flour, plus more for rolling

1 teaspoon kosher salt

8 tablespoons (1 stick) unsalted butter, cut into ½-inch cubes and chilled

¼ cup ice-cold water

1 large egg (if blind baking)

1. TO MAKE BY HAND: In a large bowl, whisk together the flour and salt. Scatter the butter over the flour and use a pastry blender or your fingers to cut the butter into the flour until it is thoroughly coated and the biggest pieces are the size of small peas. Gradually drizzle the water on top, using a rubber spatula or your hands to stir until the dough comes together. The dough should not be watery or wet.

TO MAKE IN A FOOD PROCESSOR: Pulse together the flour and salt. Sprinkle the butter over the flour and pulse until the butter is coated in flour and the biggest pieces are the size of small peas. Drizzle the water on top and pulse until the dough comes together. The dough should not be watery or wet.

2. Shape the dough into a flattened ball. Wrap it tightly in plastic wrap and refrigerate for at least 1 hour. (The dough can be tightly wrapped and frozen for up to 1 month at this point. Thaw in the refrigerator before proceeding.)

3. Lightly dust the counter with flour and roll the dough out to a round 2½ inches larger than a 9-inch pie plate or 3½ inches larger than a 9-inch deep-dish pie plate. Transfer the dough to the pie plate and carefully ease it into the edges. Trim the dough to an even ½ inch all around and fold it under itself on top of the rim. Use your fingers to crimp the crust along the rim. Refrigerate for 1 hour.

4. If the pie or quiche recipe calls for an unbaked crust, you're ready to go ahead with that recipe. If it calls for a blind-baked crust, preheat the oven to 425°F.

5. Use a fork to poke the dough several times on the bottom and sides of the pan (this is called docking). Line the chilled dough with parchment paper or foil. Fill with dried beans or pie weights, gently spreading them so that they cover the full base and the edges.

6. Bake until the edges of the dough are just beginning to brown, about 15 minutes. Remove the crust from the oven and carefully transfer the parchment or foil with the beans or weights to a large heatproof bowl. Return the crust to the oven and bake until the bottom is dry and lightly browned, about 5 minutes. Beat the egg with 1 tablespoon water in a small dish. Gently brush the egg over the bottom of the crust. Bake for 1 minute to cook the egg.

7. Let cool or proceed as directed in the recipe.

Makes one 9-inch regular or deep-dish crust

BAKED EGG BREAD PUDDING
WITH SPINACH, BOURSIN & BACON

Savory Boursin cheese is delicious with eggs. I typically use either the garlic and herb or the shallot and chive variations, but I'm sure any flavor would be fantastic here, so use your favorite. If you want to get ahead, you can do everything except the baking the night before and refrigerate the ramekins. The next morning, let them sit on the counter for 20 minutes while the oven heats up, then bake as directed. These individual servings of pudding make an elegant presentation.

PREP: *15 minutes*	COOK: *50 to 55 minutes*	COOL: *none*

Butter, for the ramekins
1 cup half-and-half
6 large eggs
4 ounces French bread, torn into bite-size pieces (about 4 cups)
4 ounces bacon, coarsely chopped

1 large shallot, finely chopped (about ¼ cup)
3 ounces baby spinach (about 3 cups)
3 ounces Boursin cheese, crumbled
2 teaspoons minced chives
Kosher salt and freshly ground black pepper

1. Preheat the oven to 350°F. Butter four 10-ounce ramekins and set them on a rimmed baking sheet, for ease of handling.

2. In a large bowl, whisk together the half-and-half and 2 of the eggs. Add the bread and stir to coat. Let stand until needed, stirring occasionally to help the bread absorb the liquid.

3. In a large skillet, cook the bacon over medium heat until crisp, about 10 minutes. Transfer the bacon with a slotted spoon to a medium bowl. Pour off all but about 2 teaspoons of the fat and reduce the heat to medium-low.

4. Stir the shallot into the skillet and cook, stirring often, until tender, about 2 minutes.

5. Add the spinach and cook, stirring often, until lightly wilted, 1 to 2 minutes. Stir into the bread mixture.

6. Add the Boursin, chives, ½ teaspoon salt, ¼ teaspoon pepper, and reserved bacon to the bread mixture and mix well. It's fine if some of the Boursin is in marble-size pieces.

7. Divide the mixture among the ramekins and bake for 15 minutes.

8. Remove the ramekins from the oven and crack an egg on top of each one. Sprinkle with salt and pepper. Continue baking until the egg whites are set, 20 to 25 minutes more. Serve at once.

Makes 4 servings

GARLIC CHEESE GRITS

Ella loves cheese grits, so I know that she's automatically going to be thrilled whenever I make these to serve with fried eggs and bacon or sausage. For my part, I love that a big bowl of warm grits fills everyone's bellies in such a satisfying way. And of course, I love cheese. As delicious as these are, unadorned grits are definitely a little pale, so they need a pretty garnish to dress them up. I like to sprinkle paprika and chives on top, because both are always in my kitchen, but let your own tastes guide your choice. Chopped parsley, freshly ground black pepper, a pat of butter, and chopped roasted peppers are some great options.

PREP: *10 minutes*	**COOK**: *45 minutes*	**COOL**: *none*

Vegetable oil spray

2½ cups quick-cooking grits

½ cup heavy cream

8 ounces processed cheese, such as Velveeta, cut into cubes

1½ cups grated sharp white Cheddar cheese (about 6 ounces)

2 teaspoons garlic powder

1 tablespoon garlic salt

1 teaspoon sweet paprika, for serving

¼ cup minced chives, for serving

1. Preheat the oven to 375°F. Spray a 9 x 13-inch baking dish with vegetable oil and set aside.

2. In a large saucepan, bring 10 cups water to a boil. Stir in the grits and reduce the heat to medium-low. Cook, stirring constantly, until tender, 4 to 5 minutes. Stir in the cream, Velveeta, Cheddar, garlic powder, and garlic salt and cook, stirring, until the cheese is melted and the mixture is well combined, about 5 minutes.

3. Pour into the prepared baking dish.

4. Bake until the top is set and golden, about 30 minutes; a few cracks might appear. Served warm, the grits will be soft and spoonable. They will firm up as they sit at room temperature. Sprinkle with paprika and chives just before serving.

5. Store leftovers in a covered container in the refrigerator for up to 2 days. To reheat, slice the grits into squares and bake in a 350°F oven until warmed through.

Makes 10 to 12 servings

SAUSAGE & HASH BROWN CASSEROLE

This savory Southern casserole contains all the fixings for a classic breakfast of eggs, sausage, and hash browns in a single dish, which makes it great for feeding a crowd. Serve it with Fresh Tomato Salsa (page 157) for extra bright color and flavor.

PREP: *10 minutes*	**COOK:** *1 hour 5 minutes*	**COOL:** *none*

Vegetable oil spray

1 pound loose breakfast sausage

1 tablespoon extra virgin olive oil, or as needed

1 small white onion, cut into ½-inch dice

One 32-ounce container frozen diced hash brown potatoes

8 large eggs

1 cup heavy cream

½ cup milk

1 teaspoon garlic powder

½ teaspoon sweet paprika

Pinch of ground sage

1 teaspoon kosher salt

½ teaspoon ground white pepper

2 cups grated sharp Cheddar cheese (about 8 ounces)

¼ cup minced chives

1. Preheat the oven to 375°F. Spray a 9 x 13-inch baking dish with vegetable oil.

2. Line a plate with paper towels. In a large skillet, cook the sausage over medium heat until browned, about 5 minutes, breaking it up with the side of a spoon. Use a slotted spoon to transfer the sausage to the paper towels. If there is very little oil left behind in the pan, add some olive oil. Sauté the onion until translucent, about 5 minutes. Stir in the hash brown potatoes and cook until the potatoes are tender, stirring occasionally, about 8 minutes. Stir in the reserved sausage. Remove the pan from the heat.

3. In a large bowl, whisk together the eggs, cream, milk, garlic powder, paprika, sage, salt, and white pepper. Whisk in the Cheddar. Stir in the sausage/hash browns mixture.

4. Pour the mixture into the prepared baking dish.

5. Bake until the top is browned and the center is set, about 45 minutes. Cover the baking dish with foil if the top begins to brown before the center is set.

6. Remove from the oven and sprinkle the chives on top before serving.

7. The casserole is best served the same day it is baked. Store leftovers in a covered container in the refrigerator for up to 2 days.

Makes 12 servings

EGGS BENEDICT CASSEROLE

Eggs Benedict is one of Chip's favorite dishes, but he tends to get it only when we go out. I think this classic is more typically a restaurant dish because it's so time consuming in a home setting to serve up a bunch of individual plates of toasted English muffins, fried Canadian bacon, poached eggs, and hollandaise sauce. But putting those ingredients in a casserole gets you all the flavor in a fraction of the time—and there's no last-minute composing. Now Chip gets his favorite breakfast and I get a lot more time to sit and enjoy it with our family.

PREP: *20 minutes*	COOK: *about 1 hour*	COOL: *none*

8 tablespoons (1 stick) salted butter, cut into ½-inch pieces, plus softened butter for the pan

12 English muffins, preferably Thomas' original, torn or cut into 1½-inch pieces

10 ounces Canadian bacon, cut into 1½-inch pieces

18 large eggs

1½ cups milk

1½ cups heavy cream

1½ teaspoons garlic powder

1½ teaspoons kosher salt

1½ teaspoons freshly ground black pepper

½ teaspoon sweet paprika

HOLLANDAISE SAUCE

8 large egg yolks

3 tablespoons fresh lemon juice, plus more if needed

¾ pound (3 sticks) salted butter, melted

Pinch of cayenne pepper

Pinch of ground white pepper

GARNISH

Sweet paprika

2 tablespoons chopped fresh parsley

1. Preheat the oven to 375°F. Generously butter a 9 x 13 x 3-inch (deep) baking dish.

2. Scatter the English muffin pieces across the prepared baking dish. Scatter the cubed butter on top, followed by the Canadian bacon.

3. In a large bowl, whisk together the eggs, milk, cream, garlic powder, salt, and pepper. Pour the egg mixture over the bread and bacon, completely covering it.

4. Cover with foil and bake for 30 minutes. Uncover and sprinkle the paprika on top. Bake until set and lightly browned, about 30 minutes.

5. Meanwhile, make the hollandaise sauce: In a medium stainless-steel bowl or the top of a double boiler, combine the egg yolks, lemon juice, and 2 tablespoons water. Nest the bowl over a pot of simmering water (the bowl should not touch the water) and whisk the mixture until the egg yolks thicken and double in volume. Whisking constantly, add the butter in a slow, steady stream. The sauce will thicken and increase in volume, 4 to 5 minutes. Add the cayenne and white pepper. Taste and add more lemon juice if needed.

6. Remove the pan from the heat. Leave the bowl over the water to keep the sauce warm.

7. Remove the casserole from the oven and pour over some warm hollandaise. Dust with some paprika and the parsley. Serve at once, passing the rest of the hollandaise at the table. The casserole is best served warm.

Makes 12 to 14 servings

FROM THE KITCHEN OF MAGNOLIA TABLE WACO, TX.

SAVORY HAM & CHEESE BREAD PUDDING
WITH TOMATO HOLLANDAISE

This yummy brunch casserole can be put together the night before and placed in the oven a few minutes before your guests arrive. Adding a bit of tomato paste to a classic hollandaise sauce gives it a lovely rosy hue and a nice tangy flavor. Sometimes I top this with some lightly dressed arugula whose peppery notes pair well with the flavors in the casserole.

PREP: *25 minutes, plus 1 hour to overnight chilling*	**COOK**: *about 1 hour*	**COOL**: *15 minutes*

Vegetable oil spray

8 large eggs

1½ cups heavy cream

2 tablespoons fresh thyme leaves

3 garlic cloves, finely chopped

1 teaspoon kosher salt

1 teaspoon mustard powder

½ teaspoon sweet paprika

½ teaspoon freshly ground black pepper

1 teaspoon ground nutmeg

One 1-pound loaf French bread, cut into ½-inch-thick slices

8 ounces thickly sliced deli Black Forest ham, chopped into bite-size pieces (about 1 cup)

8 ounces sharp Cheddar cheese, grated (about 2 cups)

2 ounces Parmesan cheese, shredded (about ½ cup)

TOMATO HOLLANDAISE SAUCE

4 large egg yolks

1½ tablespoons fresh lemon juice, plus more if needed

12 tablespoons (1½ sticks) salted butter, melted

2 teaspoons tomato paste, plus more if needed

Pinch of cayenne pepper

Pinch of ground white pepper

1. Spray a 9 x 13-inch baking dish with vegetable oil.

2. In a large bowl, whisk together the eggs and cream until well blended. Whisk in the thyme, garlic, salt, mustard, paprika, pepper, and nutmeg.

3. Trim the crusts from the bread. Line the bottom of the prepared baking dish with the bread, cutting the slices as needed to fit. Top evenly with the chopped ham and Cheddar. Cover with the rest of the bread, again cutting the slices to fit.

4. Pour the egg mixture slowly and evenly over the bread, letting it seep down between the slices. Sprinkle the Parmesan over the top.

5. Cover and refrigerate for at least 1 hour and up to overnight. Press gently from time to time to help the bread absorb the liquid.

6. Preheat the oven to 350°F.

continued . . .

continued from page 37

7. Bake until deep golden on the top and just set and a knife inserted in the center comes out moist but not wet, about 50 minutes. Cool the pan on a wire rack for at least 15 minutes before serving.

8. While the pudding is baking, make the tomato hollandaise sauce: In a medium stainless-steel bowl or the top of a double boiler, combine the egg yolks, lemon juice, and 1 tablespoon water. Nest the bowl over a pot of simmering water (the bowl should not touch the water) and whisk the mixture until the egg yolks thicken and double in volume, 3 to 4 minutes.

9. Whisking constantly, add the butter in a slow, steady stream. The sauce will thicken and increase in volume. Add the 2 teaspoons tomato paste, the cayenne, and white pepper. Stir in more tomato paste as desired for deeper flavor and color.

10. Taste and add more lemon juice if needed.

11. Serve the pudding topped with a spoonful of the tomato hollandaise sauce.

12. The casserole is best served the day it is made. Store leftovers in a covered container in the refrigerator for up to 2 days.

Makes 8 servings

VANILLA CAKE DONUTS
WITH MAPLE GLAZE

*The enticing flavors and aromas of vanilla and maple pair perfectly in
these yummy donuts. A platter of these will please any crowd.*

PREP: *30 minutes*	COOK: *45 minutes*	COOL: *none*

DONUTS

2¼ cups cake flour, plus more for the work
    surface

1 teaspoon baking powder

¼ teaspoon baking soda

¼ teaspoon kosher salt

¼ teaspoon ground nutmeg

1 large egg

½ cup buttermilk

½ cup granulated sugar

Seeds from ½ split and scraped vanilla bean or
    1 teaspoon vanilla bean paste

2 tablespoons salted butter, melted

Vegetable oil, for deep-frying

GLAZE

1 cup powdered sugar

5 to 6 tablespoons very dark maple syrup

1. To make the donuts: In a large bowl, whisk together the flour, baking powder, baking soda, salt, and nutmeg.

2. In a medium bowl, whisk together the egg, buttermilk, and granulated sugar until smooth and frothy. Whisk in the vanilla seeds or paste. Pour into the flour mixture. Add the melted butter and stir until smooth.

3. Pour onto a floured surface and knead gently to form a ball of soft, smooth dough. Pat or roll to a ½-inch thickness. Use a 2½-inch round cutter dipped in flour to stamp out as many donuts as you can, then use a 1-inch cutter dipped in flour to stamp out the center holes. Gather and roll the holes and scraps and stamp out more donuts.

4. Meanwhile, pour 2 inches of oil into a deep cast-iron skillet. Have ready a wire rack lined with paper towels to use for draining. Heat the oil to 360°F on a deep-fry thermometer.

5. Working in batches, use a slotted spoon to lower the donuts into the hot oil. Do not add more than can float freely in the hot oil. Fry the donuts until browned on both sides, flipping once, about 1 minute per side. Transfer to the rack. Continue frying the donuts, adjusting the heat as needed to keep the oil steady at 360°F.

6. To make the glaze: In a medium bowl, stir together the powdered sugar and enough syrup to form a thick glaze that slides off a spoon in a wide ribbon. Spoon the glaze over the warm donuts, letting it drip down the sides.

7. Store leftovers in an airtight container at room temperature for up to 1 day.

Makes 1 dozen donuts

OVERNIGHT FRENCH TOAST

Mornings at our house are busy, so any dish I can prep the night before and Chip can put it in the oven the next morning is a win in my book—and when it involves soaking bread in sugar and cream overnight, I call it a double win.

PREP: *20 minutes, plus overnight chilling and 30 minutes standing*	COOK: *35 to 40 minutes*	COOL: *5 to 10 minutes*

8 tablespoons (1 stick) salted butter, cold, plus 1 tablespoon softened salted butter for the baking dish

One 1-pound loaf Italian bread, cut into 1-inch-thick slices

10 large eggs

2 cups heavy cream

1 cup milk

½ cup granulated sugar

2 teaspoons pure vanilla extract

1 cup packed light brown sugar

1 cup coarsely chopped pecans

½ cup all-purpose flour

Pinch of kosher salt

1 to 2 tablespoons powdered sugar (optional)

Pure maple syrup (optional)

1. Grease a 9 x 13 x 3-inch (deep) baking dish with the 1 tablespoon softened butter. Arrange the bread slices in the baking dish in two rows, overlapping the slices.

2. In a large bowl, lightly beat the eggs. Whisk in the cream, milk, granulated sugar, and vanilla. Evenly pour the mixture over the bread. Cover and refrigerate overnight.

3. Position a rack in the upper third of the oven and preheat the oven to 375°F. Remove the baking dish from the refrigerator and let stand at room temperature for 30 minutes.

4. Place the brown sugar, pecans, flour, and salt in a medium bowl. Grate the stick of cold butter on top and mix until blended and crumbly. Sprinkle the mixture over the bread.

5. Place the baking dish in the oven and bake, uncovered, until browned and the inside is set but soft, 35 to 40 minutes. Cool slightly.

6. Dust with powdered sugar (if using). Serve warm, with maple syrup if desired.

7. The casserole is best served the day it is made. Store leftovers in a covered container in the refrigerator for up to 2 days.

Makes 12 servings

SYRIAN - ANISE BREAD - DONUTS.

ONE (1) BATCH.

8 - CUPS FLOUR.
1 - CUP SUGAR.
2 - OR MORE TEASPOONS CRUSHED ANISE SEED.
1 - TEASPOON SALT.
1 - CUP CRUSHED NUTS.(OPTIONAL)
3 - SCRAMBLED EGGS. (PUT CRUSHED NUTS IN WITH EGGS)
2 - TEASPOONS OF CINNAMON

HEAT TO LUKEWARM: ½ LB. BUTTER, 1½ CUP MILK. AFTER BUTTER
MELTS IN MILK, USE 2 PACKS SELF RISING
YEAST.POUR SMALL AMOUNT, AT A TIME, IN THE
TOP LISTED INGREDIENTS, AND MIX GOOD UNTIL
ALL OF THE LIQUID IS PUT IN. MIX WELL UNTIL
DOUGH DOES NOT STICK TO HANDS. COVER AND LET
RISE FOR ABOUT 2 HOURS.

SYRUP DIP.

1 - CUP OF WATER
¼ - STICK OF BUTTER.
¼ - CUP OF MILK.
2 - CUP OF SUGAR.
1 - TEASPOON OF VANILLA.

BOIL UNTIL LIQUID STIFFINS. KEEP STIRRING
TO KEEP FROM BURNING. MAKE THE DOUGH INTO
THE SIZE OF A GOLF BALL. ROLL THEM OUT TO
ABOUT 6 INCH'S LONG, AS A CIGAR. MAKE EACH
INTO A RING AND PRESS OUT. PLACE ON UNGREASED
COOKIE SHEET PAN. OVEN AT 350" ON LOWER SHELF
UNTIL BROWN. SWITCH OVEN TO 500' AND PLACE ON
TOP SHELF UNTIL TOP HAS TURNED BROWN.

THIS SIZE BATCH WILL MAKE ABOUT 3 DOZEN.

SYRIAN DONUTS

This recipe holds a very special place in my heart. When I was twelve years old, my grandfather invited me over to teach me how to bake this family favorite. He was a quiet man, and we rarely had the opportunity to really connect. He and my grandmother had nine kids and there were lots of grandchildren, so it was rare to spend any time alone with either of them. While we mixed the dough and shaped the donuts that day, he told me stories about his life and the history of our family that I had never heard before. It was a day I will never forget, and even though he is gone now, this recipe always makes me feel connected to him. I am forever grateful that he typed the recipe out for me that day. These subtly sweet, dense donuts have become my children's favorite weekend treat. They love to make them with me and hear me recount those stories that my grandfather told me so many years ago. Perhaps this will help them feel their own connection to an amazing man who they never had a chance to meet.

SYRIAN DONUTS

PREP: *45 minutes, plus 2 hours rising*	COOK: *about 1 hour*	COOL: *none*

8 cups all-purpose flour, plus more for the work surface

2 cups sugar (see Note)

2 to 3 teaspoons ground anise seed (see Note)

2 teaspoons ground cinnamon

1 teaspoon sea salt

3 large eggs

½ cup finely chopped walnuts

½ cup finely chopped pecans

½ pound (2 sticks) salted butter

1½ cups milk

Two ¼-ounce packets active dry yeast

SYRUP DIP

2 cups sugar

¼ cup milk

4 tablespoons (½ stick) salted butter

1 teaspoon pure vanilla extract

1 cup water

1. In a large bowl, whisk together the flour, all but 1 tablespoon of the sugar, the anise seed, cinnamon, and salt. Set aside.

2. In a medium bowl, whisk the eggs. Add the nuts and whisk to blend. Pour into the dry ingredients and stir until combined. The mixture will be dry. Set aside.

3. In a medium saucepan, melt the butter over medium heat. Add the milk and the remaining 1 tablespoon sugar and heat until the mixture is warm (105° to 115°F). Remove from the heat. Stir in the yeast and let stand until foamy, about 5 minutes.

4. Add the warm liquid to the dry ingredients and mix well (I use my hands) until the dough comes together and doesn't stick to your hands or spoon. The dough will be very dense.

5. Cover the bowl with a clean kitchen towel and let rise in a warm place for 2 hours.

6. Position an oven rack in the top third of the oven and preheat the oven to 350°F. Line a baking sheet with parchment paper.

7. Lightly flour a clean work surface. Pull a golf ball–size piece of dough out of the bowl and place it on the floured surface. Use your hands to roll it into a 6-inch-long "cigar" and then curve it into a round donut. Seal the ends together where they meet. Place on the lined baking sheet and flatten it with your hand. Continue making donuts, placing them 1 inch apart on the sheet.

8. Bake until lightly browned on top, about 15 minutes. Repeat with remaining dough.

9. Meanwhile, make the syrup dip: In a medium saucepan, combine the sugar, milk, butter, vanilla, and water. Bring to a boil over medium-high heat, then reduce the heat and simmer until the syrup is clear and thickens slightly, 7 to 10 minutes.

continued . . .

continued from page 45

10. Line a baking sheet with wax paper. Dunk both sides of the warm donuts in the syrup and lay them on the wax paper to set. Serve the donuts warm.

11. Store the donuts in an airtight container at room temperature for up to 2 days.

Makes about 3 dozen donuts

NOTE: *You may notice that my grandfather's recipe (pictured on page 42) calls for just 1 cup of sugar. I like everything sweeter, so I always use 2 cups. I love anise seed so I always use the larger amount. Not everyone likes so much of this unusual spice, so use the smaller amount if you prefer.*

BACON & GRUYÈRE DROP BISCUITS

I like to serve these savory biscuits warm out of the oven with Bacon-Tomato Sweet Drip Jam (page 82) or blackberry jam, alongside fried eggs and sliced fruit. They also make a great hors d'oeuvre for a cocktail party (see Note).

PREP: *15 minutes*	**COOK:** *40 to 45 minutes*	**COOL:** *5 minutes*

½ pound thick-sliced peppered bacon
1½ cups all-purpose flour
2 teaspoons baking powder
1 teaspoon garlic powder
1 teaspoon garlic salt
1 teaspoon kosher salt

½ teaspoon ground white pepper
8 tablespoons (1 stick) unsalted butter, cut into cubes
¾ cup milk
8 ounces Gruyère cheese, grated (about 2 cups)

1. Preheat the oven to 400°F.

2. Arrange the bacon slices on a baking sheet. Bake until crispy, about 20 minutes. Line a second baking sheet with paper towels and transfer the bacon to the paper towels to drain. Set aside.

3. Line another baking sheet with parchment paper.

4. In a food processor, combine the flour, baking powder, garlic powder, garlic salt, salt, and white pepper. Pulse a few times to combine. Scatter the butter on top of the flour and pulse until the dough resembles coarse pebbles.

5. Transfer the mixture to a large bowl and add the milk and Gruyère. Crumble the bacon into the bowl. Mix with your hands just until the dough comes together. Don't overmix.

6. Use a 4-ounce ice cream scoop to drop uniform biscuit mounds on the prepared baking sheet. Bake until the edges are crispy, 20 to 25 minutes. Let cool slightly in the pan on a rack.

7. Biscuits are best the day they are made, but leftovers can be stored in an airtight container at room temperature for up to 2 days. Warm in a preheated 300°F oven.

Makes 6 biscuits

NOTE: *To make smaller drop biscuits to serve as hors d'oeuvres, use a 2-ounce scoop and bake them for the same amount of time as instructed above.*

THE BEST-EVER FLUFFY PANCAKES

*A long time ago a friend of mine shared with me this recipe from her grandmother.
We eat a lot of pancakes around here—there's a reason there are two recipes for them
in this book—and I always have a boxed mix in the pantry for when I just don't have
the time to make them from scratch. But on the mornings when I do have those extra
few minutes, it's so worth it.*

PREP: *10 minutes, plus 20 to 30 minutes resting*	**COOK**: *under 15 minutes*	**COOL**: *none*

2 cups all-purpose flour

¼ cup sugar

1 tablespoon baking powder

2 teaspoons baking soda

1 teaspoon kosher salt

2 cups buttermilk

½ cup plus 2 tablespoons vegetable oil or melted bacon grease or 10 tablespoons (1¼ sticks) unsalted butter, melted, plus vegetable oil for the skillet

2 large eggs

Salted butter, for serving

Pure maple syrup, for serving

1. In a large bowl, whisk together the flour, sugar, baking powder, baking soda, and salt. Set aside.

2. In a medium bowl, whisk together the buttermilk, oil, and eggs.

3. Pour the liquid ingredients into the flour mixture and stir together until well combined. Let stand for 20 to 30 minutes. The batter will begin to get fluffy.

4. Heat a skillet or griddle over medium-high heat until hot. Generously oil the hot skillet. When a few droplets of water carefully splashed on the surface sizzle, pour ¼ cup batter per pancake into the pan, far enough apart that the pancakes don't touch.

5. Cook until lightly browned on the bottom and the top is bubbly, about 2 minutes. Flip and cook until lightly browned on the other side, about 2 minutes. Transfer to a platter. Repeat to make the rest of the pancakes, adding more oil to the pan if necessary.

6. Serve hot, with butter and maple syrup.

7. Pancakes are best eaten hot just after cooking.

Makes 4 servings

RICOTTA PANCAKES

Ricotta makes these pancakes especially moist and a generous amount of vanilla makes them taste and smell amazing. This is one of the showstoppers on the menu at Magnolia Table.

PREP: *10 minutes*	**COOK**: *under 15 minutes*	**COOL**: *none*

2 cups all-purpose flour
¼ cup sugar
1 teaspoon baking soda
2 cups milk
¾ cup ricotta cheese

2 large eggs
1 tablespoon pure vanilla extract
8 tablespoons (1 stick) salted butter, or as needed, plus more for serving
Pure maple syrup, for serving

1. In a large bowl, whisk together the flour, sugar, and baking soda.

2. In a medium bowl, whisk together the milk, ricotta, eggs, and vanilla until well blended.

3. Add the wet ingredients to the dry ingredients and stir until just combined.

4. Heat a large skillet over medium heat until hot. Add 2 tablespoons butter to the hot skillet and swirl the pan to coat with melted butter.

5. Pour the batter about ¼ cup at a time to form as many pancakes as will fit without crowding. Cook until the tops are covered with bubbles and the edges are crispy brown, about 3 minutes. Then flip and cook for 2 to 3 minutes on the other side, until browned on the bottom. Transfer the pancakes to a platter.

6. Repeat to cook the rest of the pancakes. Serve hot with butter and maple syrup.

7. Pancakes are best eaten hot just after cooking.

Makes 4 servings

QUICK ORANGE-WALNUT SWEET ROLLS

I think it's fair to say that I crave sweet cinnamon rolls pretty much all the time. For years I thought I had no choice but to live with this craving because there was no way to make delicious rolls at home without yeasted dough. The fact that you have to let the dough rise for a couple hours disqualifies them from our regular weekday morning rotation and even from most weekends. One of the happiest epiphanies I ever had was when it occurred to me that I could use refrigerated crescent dough instead. Now whenever that craving becomes too loud to ignore, I make these.

PREP: *20 minutes*	**COOK**: *30 minutes*	**COOL**: *5 minutes*

ROLLS

12 tablespoons (1½ sticks) salted butter, at room temperature
¾ cup packed light brown sugar
4 teaspoons lightly packed finely grated orange zest
1 teaspoon ground cinnamon
Two 8-ounce cans refrigerated crescent rolls
1 cup chopped walnuts

GLAZE

2 cups powdered sugar, sifted
Finely grated zest of 2 oranges
2 teaspoons pure vanilla extract
¼ to ½ cup fresh orange juice

1. Preheat the oven to 375°F.

2. To make the rolls: In a medium bowl, place the butter, brown sugar, orange zest, and cinnamon and use a large fork to mash the mixture into a paste.

3. Open one can of crescent dough and unroll the dough onto a work surface. Press all the perforations closed to make a single rectangle. Spread half the butter mixture evenly over the dough. Scatter half the walnuts over the butter. Starting with one long side, roll up the rectangle to form a log. Repeat with the remaining can of dough, butter mixture, and walnuts.

4. Cut each log crosswise into 6 pieces. Arrange the pieces cut side up in an 8-inch round cake pan.

5. Bake until deep golden on top, about 30 minutes.

6. Meanwhile, make the glaze: In a medium bowl, whisk together the powdered sugar, orange zest, and vanilla. Whisk in enough orange juice to make a soft glaze that drips in a wide ribbon off the whisk.

7. Invert the warm rolls onto a serving plate and let stand 5 minutes. Drizzle the glaze over the rolls. Serve warm.

8. Store in an airtight container at room temperature for up to 2 days.

Makes 12 sweet rolls

CINNAMON SWIRL & WALNUT QUICK BREAD
WITH CRUNCHY WALNUT TOPPING

This fantastic quick bread is so easy to prepare, and it's especially delicious with a big mug of hot coffee or a tall glass of milk for the kids.

PREP: *25 minutes*	COOK: *45 to 50 minutes*	COOL: *1 hour*

TOPPING
¼ cup packed light brown sugar
1 tablespoon all-purpose flour
½ teaspoon ground cinnamon
1 tablespoon salted butter, melted
¼ cup chopped walnuts

FILLING
½ cup granulated sugar
1 tablespoon ground cinnamon

CAKE
Nonstick baking spray or vegetable shortening, for the pan

2 cups all-purpose flour
1 cup granulated sugar
1 teaspoon baking soda
½ teaspoon kosher salt
1 cup buttermilk
1 large egg
¼ cup vegetable oil
2 teaspoons pure vanilla extract
½ cup chopped walnuts

GLAZE
¼ cup powdered sugar
1 to 2 teaspoons milk

1. To make the topping: In a small bowl, whisk together the brown sugar, flour, and cinnamon. Stir in the melted butter, then the walnuts. Refrigerate until needed.

2. To make the filling: In a small bowl, whisk together the granulated sugar and cinnamon. Set aside until needed.

3. To make the cake: Preheat the oven to 350°F. Spray a 9 x 5-inch loaf pan with nonstick baking spray or lightly grease with vegetable shortening.

4. In a large bowl, whisk together the flour, granulated sugar, baking soda, and salt.

5. In a medium bowl, whisk together the buttermilk, egg, oil, and vanilla. Form a well in the flour mixture, pour in the buttermilk mixture, and stir only until smooth. Fold in the walnuts.

6. Scrape half the batter (about 1½ cups) into the prepared pan. Sprinkle the reserved filling evenly over the batter. Scrape in the rest of the batter and smooth the top. Use a skewer or the tip of a long knife to cut through the batter up and back in an S shape to create a swirl pattern.

7. Sprinkle the reserved topping evenly over the top.

8. Bake until a tester inserted in the center comes out clean, 45 to 50 minutes. Shield the top with a flat sheet of foil if it browns too quickly.

9. Cool in the pan on a wire rack for 10 minutes, then remove the loaf from the pan, turn upright, and cool to room temperature.

10. To make the glaze: In a small bowl, whisk the powdered sugar to remove lumps. Whisk in enough milk, a few drops at a time, to make a thick, smooth glaze that drips off the whisk. Drizzle over the cooled loaf.

11. Tightly wrap the bread in foil and store at room temperature for up to 3 days.

Makes 8 servings

ORANGE SCONES

It's fun to make these with the kids, because there are tasks for the littlest as well as the biggest, from whisking together ingredients to working the orange zest into the sugar (a job that's fun and smells really good). When giving these to friends, pack the glaze separately in a glass jar so they can spoon it over the scones themselves.

PREP: *25 minutes*	**COOK**: *about 15 minutes*	**COOL**: *5 minutes*

2 cups all-purpose flour, plus more for forming the scones

1½ teaspoons baking powder

½ teaspoon baking soda

½ teaspoon kosher salt

1 large egg

¾ cup sour cream

½ cup sugar

1 teaspoon grated orange zest

12 tablespoons (1½ sticks) unsalted butter, cut into 1-inch cubes and frozen

MAPLE-ORANGE GLAZE

1¾ cups powdered sugar

1 teaspoon grated orange zest

3 tablespoons unsalted butter, melted

3 tablespoons fresh orange juice

1 teaspoon pure vanilla extract

½ teaspoon pure maple syrup

1. Preheat the oven to 400°F. Line a baking sheet with parchment paper.

2. In a large bowl, whisk together the flour, baking powder, baking soda, and salt. Set aside.

3. In a small bowl, lightly whisk the egg. Whisk in the sour cream. Set aside.

4. In another small bowl, place the sugar and orange zest. Using the back of a spoon, work the zest into the sugar until well combined. Stir the sugar mixture into the flour mixture. Add the frozen butter and, using your fingers or a pastry blender, blend until the mixture is pebble-like. Stir in the egg/sour cream mixture until the dough forms a ball (use your hands if it's easier). Divide the dough in half.

5. Place one dough portion on a lightly floured surface and press it into a 6-inch round. (It should be about ¾ to 1 inch thick.) Cut the round into 6 wedges. Arrange the wedges 1 inch apart on the prepared baking sheet. Repeat with the second dough portion.

6. Bake until golden, 13 to 15 minutes. Cool on the baking sheet for 5 minutes, then transfer the scones to a wire rack set on a baking sheet.

7. Meanwhile, make the maple-orange glaze: In a medium bowl, stir together the powdered sugar and orange zest. Stir in the melted butter, orange juice, vanilla, and maple syrup, mixing until smooth.

8. Spoon the glaze over the scones. Serve the scones warm or at room temperature. Once glazed, the scones are best eaten the same day. Store unglazed leftovers in an airtight container at room temperature for up to 3 days.

Makes 12 scones

CINNAMON SQUARES

These are, hands down, my kids' favorite breakfast. Who am I kidding? They're my favorite, too, especially when served alongside eggs—I can't get enough of that combination of sweet and salty. These are definitely a labor of love, but honestly I think we all enjoy preparing them almost as much as we like to eat them. I'm in my happy place anytime I get to work with dough. Mixing the ingredients together into a cohesive whole, draping a towel over the bowl and letting the dough rise, punching it down, and then rolling, filling, and shaping it—the ritual of every step brings me pure joy. Whenever I bust out the ingredients for these squares, the kids know it's a good day. I make these a lot during school holidays when there's time in the morning for them to help. Duke and Emmie stand at attention with the measured ingredients waiting for the sign from me that they can dump them into the bowl, and then the older two help me roll out the dough and compose each layer. Drake loves that he's finally allowed to use a big knife to cut the squares before they're baked, and then he and Ella apply the egg wash to the tops of them. The kids understand that the bit of extra effort required for these squares makes them something really special.

I think it probably helps that these squares are the best iteration of a cinnamon roll that any of us has ever tasted. It can be hard to get a good balance with cinnamon rolls—they either have too much bread or too much cinnamon. The way I make these, rolling and folding them repeatedly so that the filling is between several thin layers of dough, results in a square that has a perfect amount of both bread and cinnamon, so every bite is balanced.

CINNAMON SQUARES

PREP: *45 minutes, plus 1 hour rising*	COOK: *25 to 30 minutes*	COOL: *none*

DOUGH

¼ cup warm water (105° to 115°F)

Two ¼-ounce packets active dry yeast

2 cups sugar

1¼ cups milk, warmed

8 tablespoons (1 stick) salted butter, melted and cooled, plus softened butter for the dough and pans

2 large eggs, beaten

1 teaspoon kosher salt

6 cups all-purpose flour, plus more for dusting

FILLING

2 cups pecan halves

½ pound (2 sticks) salted butter, cut into pieces and chilled

2 cups packed light brown sugar

2 teaspoons ground cinnamon

EGG WASH

1 large egg, beaten

1. In a large bowl, stir together the water, yeast, and 1 tablespoon sugar. Let stand until foamy, 3 to 4 minutes. Add the remaining sugar, milk, butter, eggs, and salt and stir with a wooden spoon until well blended. Add the flour and stir until the dough comes together. Rub softened butter on top of the dough and around the bowl. Cover and let stand in a warm spot for 1 hour.

2. To make the filling: In a food processor, combine the pecans, butter, brown sugar, and cinnamon and process until the mixture is well blended and paste-like (do this in two batches if necessary).

3. Position a rack in the middle of the oven and preheat the oven to 350°F. Line a baking sheet with parchment paper.

4. Generously dust a work surface with flour. Punch down the dough and place it on the work surface. Roll it out into a 16 x 24-inch rectangle. (See photos a and b.)

5. Spoon two-thirds of the filling mixture over the dough. Spread it to cover the dough to the edges. (See photo c.) Starting on a short side, fold the sheet of dough in half, pressing the two short sides together to make sure they stick together and to flatten it slightly (you'll have a roughly 14 x 16-inch rectangle). (See photo d.)

6. Spoon the remaining filling on top of the dough and spread it to cover the dough. Starting at a short side, fold the dough in half, bringing the two short sides together to cover the filling. Use your hands to flatten the rectangle and "smoosh" it into an approximately 12 x 18-inch rectangle. (See photos e, f, and g.)

7. Use a chef's knife to cut the dough into 24 roughly 3-inch squares. (See photos h and i.) Arrange the squares on the prepared pan so that they are touching. Brush the tops of the squares with beaten egg.

8. Bake until lightly golden, 25 to 30 minutes. Serve hot.

9. Store in an airtight container at room temperature for up to 2 days.

Makes 24 squares

AFTER-SCHOOL BANANA BREAD

I always buy a big bunch of bananas on Monday, and typically by the end of the week there are some that have just a few too many brown spots for my kids to eat them. I turn those into this quick bread and either serve it for breakfast with scrambled eggs or leave it on the stove for them to eat when they get home from school. Their tradition is to cut a slice, place a pat of butter on it, and put it in the microwave for 15 seconds so the butter melts a bit. I've made it so many times since they were small that they consider it a kitchen staple, like eggs or milk. I find that as they get older, they love the familiarity of their favorites. Often when I try something new, they're polite about it but then they'll ask me where the thing I always make for them is, because that's what they really want. They can't articulate it right now, but I think to them the comfort of home is all about their favorite dishes. Home is having banana bread on the stove when they get home from school at least one day a week. It's just what they know, and it's fun to provide that for them.

I bake my banana bread in a square pan instead of a loaf pan because I prefer the consistent texture that results. This comes out moist and just lightly browned all over. Sprinkling a bit of sugar on top just before baking adds a crunchy texture that the kids love.

AFTER-SCHOOL BANANA BREAD

PREP: *15 minutes*	**COOK**: *45 to 50 minutes*	**COOL**: *5 to 10 minutes*

Nonstick baking spray, for the pan

8 tablespoons (1 stick) salted butter, melted and cooled, plus softened butter for serving

1 cup packed light brown sugar

2 large eggs, beaten

1½ teaspoons pure vanilla extract

4 to 5 very ripe bananas, mashed (I like to leave them a little chunky)

1¾ cups all-purpose flour

1 teaspoon baking soda

½ teaspoon kosher salt

½ cup chopped pecans (optional; see Tip)

1 to 2 tablespoons granulated sugar as needed

1. Preheat the oven to 350°F. Spray an 8 x 8-inch pan with nonstick baking spray or line it with parchment paper.

2. In a stand mixer fitted with the paddle attachment (or in a large bowl with a handheld electric mixer), beat together the butter, brown sugar, eggs, and vanilla until well blended. Add the bananas and mix until combined.

3. In a medium bowl, whisk together the flour, baking soda, and salt. Add the dry ingredients to the wet ingredients and beat just until combined. Add the pecans (if using) and mix until combined.

4. Pour the batter into the prepared pan and spread it evenly. Sprinkle the sugar over the top. I like to cover the whole surface completely with sugar; use as much as you'd like.

5. Bake until a tester inserted in the center comes out clean, 45 to 50 minutes. Let the bread cool slightly in the pan on a rack. Slice and serve warm with butter.

6. When completely cooled, cover the pan with foil and store at room temperature for up to 2 days.

Makes 8 servings

TIP: *I have a friend who replaces the pecans with a cup of chocolate chips. She has declared her variation heavenly, but I think my kids might find it to be another unwelcome riff on something they consider perfect just as it is. Nonetheless, I share this tip with you to encourage riffing of your own.*

- CHAPTER 2 -

Lunch

LUNCH

During the week, our family, probably like many other families, lunches on simple sandwiches and leftovers. And while this isn't the meal I dream about, I sure get grumpy midday if I don't love what I'm eating. I just enjoy food too much to waste a meal each day on something that isn't *really* great.

That's why I'm particularly excited about the recipes in this chapter. They're super flexible, and I usually make them on the weekends to serve then and beyond. The great thing about a number of them, like the chicken salad and the pimiento cheese, is that they keep well in the fridge and they're portable. That means I can make a big batch so that there's enough to enjoy on the weekend as well as have leftovers for early in the week. Come Monday, I'll put fresh greens in one container and some leftovers in another container and I've got really great on-the-go lunches for the family in just a couple of minutes. For us, the middle of the day is almost always a very busy time, so having these adaptable, convenient foods on hand makes it less likely we'll order lunch out and instead enjoy something good from our own kitchen. Many of the recipes in this chapter are also good travelers, which makes them ideal for picnics or school lunches. I even bring many of them to showers and potlucks.

On the weekends we also like to have friends over for a leisurely late lunch, and something like the Gaines brother burgers is both relaxed and satisfying. If it's my mom who's coming over, or some of my girlfriends, I might make something like my fresh sweet pepper and pancetta frittata instead. All of these dishes can also be served as a simple dinner. I'm always amazed at the level of enthusiasm I get from Chip and the kids when I put out a big platter of BLTs or my version of grilled cheese with Havarti, tomato, and basil sandwiches. On a Saturday evening after a busy day of chores, errands, and kids' sporting events, this meal that is both simple and yummy feels like a win on every level.

BLT SANDWICHES

The combination of smoky bacon, crisp lettuce, and sweet, juicy tomato slices is a classic for a reason. Here it's made even more delicious by a couple of quick and easy embellishments. Spreading mayonnaise on the bread and toasting it on the stovetop give it a perfectly brown crust without drying out the slices. And an herb-and-lemon mayonnaise marries all the elements together beautifully.

PREP: *15 minutes*	COOK: *30 minutes*	COOL: *none*

20 thick slices applewood-smoked or peppered bacon (about 1½ pounds)

¼ cup mayonnaise, preferably Hellmann's

8 thick-cut slices white country bread

½ cup Easy Herb Mayo (page 77)

8 large butter lettuce leaves

3 vine-ripened tomatoes, sliced

Kosher salt and freshly ground black pepper

1. Preheat the oven to 400°F.

2. Arrange the bacon slices on one or two baking sheets. Bake until desired crispness is reached, about 20 minutes. Line another baking sheet with paper towels and transfer the bacon to the paper towels to drain.

3. Spread a small amount of plain mayonnaise on both sides of each slice of bread. Heat a skillet over medium heat and toast the bread on both sides until crispy and brown, 1 to 2 minutes per side.

4. Lay out 4 slices of the toast and spread each with 1 tablespoon of the herb mayo. Layer lettuce, bacon, and tomato slices on top and season to taste with salt and pepper. Spread each of the remaining 4 slices of toast with 1 tablespoon herb mayo and place mayo-side down on the toppings to form four BLTs. Slice each in half and serve.

Makes 4 servings

FROM THE KITCHEN OF
MAGNOLIA TABLE
WACO, TX.

EASY HERB MAYO

Fresh herbs and lemon juice transform regular mayonnaise into a zesty spread that elevates every sandwich it's used in. In addition to the BLT, try it with smoked turkey and cheese on a toasted brioche bun or mix it with cooked shredded chicken for a quick chicken salad. Working salt into the garlic and turning it into a paste mellows its sharp bite and makes it easier to completely incorporate into the mayonnaise. Chill the mayonnaise in the refrigerator for a couple of hours to allow the flavors to meld and the fresh herbs to really stand out.

PREP: *10 minutes, plus 2 hours chilling*	**COOK**: *none*	**COOL**: *none*

1 cup mayonnaise, preferably Hellmann's
1 small garlic clove
½ teaspoon kosher salt
2 tablespoons minced chives
1 tablespoon minced fresh flat-leaf parsley

1 tablespoon minced fresh dill
1½ teaspoons fresh lemon juice
½ teaspoon sweet paprika
½ teaspoon ground white pepper

1. Place the mayonnaise in a medium bowl. Mince the garlic on a cutting board, then add a couple of pinches of the salt to it. Tilt the knife at an angle, and scrape it over the mixture several times to work it into a paste. Add it to the mayonnaise along with the rest of the salt, the chives, parsley, dill, lemon juice, paprika, and white pepper. Stir until well combined.

2. Cover and refrigerate for 2 hours before serving.

3. Store in a covered container in the refrigerator for up to 3 days.

Makes about 1 cup

CURRY CHICKEN SALAD

WITH TOASTED NUTS

*I like to serve this unique take on chicken salad for lunch on hearty multigrain toast
or with sliced cucumber and red onion in a fresh pita. For a pretty appetizer, spoon the salad
onto endive leaves, arrange them in a spoke pattern on a platter, and sprinkle over the almonds
and chives. The amount of curry powder called for here might look like a lot but it's what makes
this taste so good. If you want to be sure, whisk just half of it into the mayonnaise and taste
before adding the rest. Water chestnuts add a satisfying crunch; you can replace them with
1 cup diced celery or jicama. Chill the salad for 2 hours for the best flavor.*

PREP: *15 minutes, plus 2 hours chilling*	COOK: *none*	COOL: *none*

6 cups shredded meat from store-bought rotisserie chicken or Poached Chicken Breasts (page 85)

One 8-ounce can diced water chestnuts, drained

1 cup chopped or sliced almonds, toasted (see below)

½ cup minced chives

2 cups mayonnaise, preferably Hellmann's

2 tablespoons soy sauce

3 tablespoons curry powder

½ teaspoon garlic powder

½ teaspoon kosher salt

½ teaspoon ground white pepper

One 1-pound loaf hearty bread, cut into ½-inch-thick slices and toasted

Endive leaves (optional)

1. In a large bowl, combine the chicken, water chestnuts, toasted almonds, and chives (hold back a few almonds and chives for garnish). Toss to combine evenly, then set aside.

2. In a medium bowl, whisk together the mayonnaise, soy sauce, curry powder, garlic powder, salt, and white pepper. Pour over the chicken and stir until well combined.

3. Cover and refrigerate for 2 hours before serving. Sprinkle the chicken salad with the reserved almonds and chives and serve with toast and endive leaves (if using).

4. Store in a covered container in the refrigerator for up to 3 days.

Makes 6 servings

FROM THE KITCHEN OF MAGNOLIA TABLE WACO, TX.

TOASTING NUTS & SESAME SEEDS

TO TOAST ON THE STOVETOP: Place the nuts or seeds in a single layer in a dry skillet over medium heat and toast, stirring frequently, until lightly browned and fragrant, 4 to 8 minutes. Immediately transfer the nuts or seeds to a plate to cool.

TO TOAST IN THE OVEN: Preheat the oven to 350°F. Spread the nuts or seeds on a rimmed baking sheet and toast in the oven, shaking the pan once or twice, until lightly browned and fragrant, 10 to 12 minutes. Immediately transfer the nuts or seeds to a plate to cool.

GAINES BROTHER BURGERS

WITH DRIP JAM

We serve this burger at Magnolia Table and I have to confess that it's one of my favorite things on the menu. My boys love burgers of just about any kind, so I could probably get away with serving something a little plainer to them (and of course you can leave any part of this out if you have picky eaters—or let everyone pick their own toppings). I just love how a grilled buttered brioche bun holds a savory burger, sweet drip jam, creamy melted cheese, and peppery fresh arugula so that every single bite is an amazing combination of flavors and textures.

PREP: *15 minutes*	COOK: *under 25 minutes*	COOL: *none*

Vegetable oil, for the grill
4 pounds ground beef (80% lean; see Note)
1 tablespoon kosher salt
1 tablespoon freshly ground black pepper
4 ounces Gruyère cheese, thinly sliced
3 garlic cloves, minced

8 tablespoons (1 stick) salted butter, melted
6 brioche buns, split
1 to 1½ cups Bacon-Tomato Sweet Drip Jam or Jalapeño Drip Jam (pages 82–83)
6 thick slices vine-ripened tomato
5 cups baby arugula (about 5 ounces)

1. Prepare a hot grill and oil the grill grate.

2. In a large bowl, combine the beef, salt, and pepper. Using your hands, gently mix the seasonings into the meat, then form 6 equal patties, each about 4½ inches across.

3. Grill the burgers for 6 to 8 minutes, then flip them and cook on the second side for 6 to 8 minutes for medium-rare to medium, as desired. During the last 2 minutes of cooking, place a few slices of Gruyère on each burger.

4. Stir the garlic into the melted butter and brush it on the insides of the buns. Grill the buns buttered side down until toasted. Flip and lightly grill the outsides, about 30 seconds.

5. Spread some drip jam on the bottom halves of the buns. Top each with a thick tomato slice, a burger, more drip jam, and some arugula. Put the tops of the buns in place and serve immediately.

Makes 6 servings

NOTE: *I usually buy grass-fed beef because I like the flavor, but you can use whatever you prefer.*

BACON-TOMATO SWEET DRIP JAM

Chip adores anything that involves bacon or jam, and this exceptional mixture is a sweet-and-savory combination of both. Drip jam is a little looser than regular jam, so it spreads beautifully when it's used as a topping, as it is on the Gaines Brother Burgers. It's also great on my homemade biscuits (page 18), served with crackers and creamy Brie, folded into risotto, or served over grits or baked polenta.

PREP: *10 minutes*	**COOK:** *1 hour 10 minutes*	**COOL:** *5 to 10 minutes*

1 pound sliced bacon, cut into ½-inch-wide pieces

1½ pounds pork belly, cut into ¼-inch dice

1 tablespoon unsalted butter

1 garlic clove, minced

1 medium white onion, cut into ½-inch dice

2 large vine-ripened tomatoes, cut into ½-inch dice

1 cup packed light brown sugar

1. In a cast-iron or other heavy skillet, cook the bacon over medium-high heat, stirring often, until crispy, about 10 minutes. Line a large platter with paper towels and transfer the bacon to the paper towels to drain.

2. Pour the grease out of the skillet and return it to medium-high heat. Add the pork belly and fry on all sides until crispy, about 15 minutes. Transfer to the paper towels to drain.

3. In a large saucepan, melt the butter over medium heat. Add the garlic and sauté until lightly browned, about 10 seconds. Add the onion and cook, stirring often, until well browned, about 10 minutes.

4. Add the reserved bacon and pork belly, tomatoes, brown sugar, and ½ cup water and stir to combine. Bring to a simmer. Reduce the heat to low and simmer gently, stirring occasionally, until the mixture is flavorful and coats the back of a spoon, about 35 minutes. Let cool slightly before using.

5. Store in a covered container in the refrigerator for up to 1 week.

Makes about 3 cups

JALAPEÑO DRIP JAM

*Spicy heat and sweet are surprisingly delicious together. Even my kids adore this jam,
especially when I spoon it over a block of cream cheese and serve it with crackers and toast.*

PREP: *5 minutes*	**COOK**: *40 minutes*	**COOL**: *5 to 10 minutes*

4 tablespoons (½ stick) unsalted butter
1 medium white onion, cut into ¼-inch dice
1 cup packed light brown sugar

One 4-ounce can diced jalapeños, undrained
  (about ½ cup)
2 tablespoons stone-ground mustard

1. In a medium saucepan, melt the butter over medium heat. Add the onion and sauté until
translucent and tender, about 6 minutes. Add the brown sugar, jalapeños with their juice, and
mustard. Stir and cook until bubbling. Reduce the heat slightly and simmer until the mixture is
flavorful and thick enough to coat the back of a spoon, about 30 minutes.

2. Let cool slightly before using. Store in a covered container in the refrigerator for up to 1 week.

Makes about 1½ cups

CHICKEN SALAD CROISSANT SANDWICHES

The sweet-and-salty combination that I love so much is particularly delectable in this savory chicken salad made with red grapes, pecans, and green onions. My kids love it on a croissant or with their favorite crackers. I like that it keeps well in the fridge so the next day I can pack it up for a quick, healthy, and very satisfying lunch at work.

PREP: *15 minutes, plus 1 to 2 hours chilling*	**COOK**: *none*	**COOL**: *none*

5 cups shredded meat from store-bought rotisserie chicken or Poached Chicken Breasts (page 85)

1½ cups halved red grapes

¾ cup chopped pecans (optional)

¼ cup thinly sliced green onions (light and dark green parts) or chives

1¼ cups mayonnaise, preferably Hellmann's

Kosher salt and freshly ground black pepper

12 small croissants, sliced horizontally in half

6 butter lettuce leaves

2 vine-ripened tomatoes, thinly sliced

1. Combine the chicken, grapes, pecans (if using), and green onions in a large bowl and toss to combine. Add the mayonnaise and salt and pepper to taste and stir until well coated.

2. Cover and chill until cold, 1 to 2 hours. Taste for seasoning. Serve on the small croissants with lettuce leaves and tomato slices.

3. Store the chicken salad in a covered container in the refrigerator for up to 3 days.

Makes 6 servings

POACHED CHICKEN BREASTS

This is a quick and easy way to cook chicken breasts to use in chicken salad, casseroles, pasta dishes, soups, or wherever cooked chicken is called for.

PREP: *5 minutes*	**COOK**: *about 15 minutes*	**COOL**: *30 minutes*

Five 8-ounce boneless, skinless chicken breasts
1 lemon, thinly sliced
1 garlic clove, smashed
1 bay leaf

One 32-ounce box chicken broth, 4 cups Homemade Chicken Broth (page 216), or water, or as needed
1 teaspoon kosher salt (optional)

1. Arrange the chicken in a single layer in a wide skillet or large Dutch oven with a tight-fitting lid. Add the lemon, garlic, and bay leaf. Pour the broth on top. If the chicken is not fully covered, add more broth or water until it is covered by at least 1 inch. Add salt if using water or unseasoned broth.

2. Bring to a boil over medium-high heat. Reduce the heat to a simmer, cover, and cook until the chicken is tender and fully cooked (165°F on an instant-read thermometer), about 8 minutes.

3. Remove the chicken from the poaching liquid and let cool completely, then shred. If desired, strain the poaching liquid and use it as a broth in another recipe.

4. Store the chicken in a tightly covered container in the refrigerator for up to 4 days. Store the strained broth in a tightly covered container in the refrigerator for up to 3 days or in the freezer for up to 2 months.

Makes about 5 cups shredded chicken

FLATBREAD PIZZA

WITH PROSCIUTTO & NEW POTATOES

This elegant and very tasty flatbread is deceptively easy to pull together, which makes it perfect for a Sunday afternoon garden party with friends. Serve it with Layered Arugula Salad with Pear Vinaigrette (page 121) or Roasted Cauliflower Soup (page 104).

PREP: *15 minutes*	**COOK**: *45 minutes*	**COOL**: *none*

Kosher salt

2 medium or 4 small red or white new potatoes (about 6 ounces)

1 tablespoon salted butter

1 garlic clove, minced

2 tablespoons all-purpose flour

1 cup heavy cream

½ cup crumbled Gorgonzola cheese (about 2 ounces)

Freshly ground black pepper or ground white pepper

One 10-inch prepared flatbread crust

1 tablespoon extra virgin olive oil

6 slices prosciutto (about 3 ounces)

¼ cup grated Parmesan cheese (about ½ ounce)

5 basil leaves, torn

1. Preheat the oven to 375°F. Line a baking sheet with parchment paper.

2. Bring a large pot of salted water to a boil. Add the potatoes, reduce the heat, and simmer until tender, 6 to 10 minutes, depending on their size. Drain and let cool. Thinly slice and set aside.

3. In a small saucepan, melt the butter over medium-low heat. Add the garlic and sauté until softened, about 30 seconds. Stir in the flour and cook for 30 seconds. Whisk in the cream and cook, stirring frequently, until warmed through and thickened, 6 to 8 minutes. Stir in the Gorgonzola until melted. Season with salt and pepper to taste. Remove from the heat.

4. Place the flatbread on the prepared baking sheet and brush it with the olive oil. Spoon the Gorgonzola cream on the crust and spread it almost to the edges.

5. Lay the prosciutto on top. Layer the sliced potatoes over the prosciutto, tucking a few of them under the strips. Dust with the Parmesan.

6. Bake until toasted and bubbling, 12 to 15 minutes. Sprinkle the basil on top. Cut into pieces and serve hot.

Makes 4 servings

1919 PIMIENTO CHEESE

We opened our restaurant, Magnolia Table, in a space with a lot of history. The building was the second location of a longtime Waco restaurant, the Elite Café, which originally opened downtown in 1919. While researching the rich past of the previous tenants, we were excited to find pimiento cheese listed on a menu that dated from the earliest days of the restaurant, back when they still used iceboxes. They didn't install refrigerators until the early 1920s— we can't even imagine trying to run a restaurant without refrigerators. For best results, use good-quality bagged shredded Cheddar because it is drier than most block Cheddar cheese and doesn't clump together when the mayonnaise is added. For a quick lunch plate, serve a couple spoonfuls of pimiento cheese with a handful of cucumber slices, celery sticks, baby radishes, and cherry tomatoes. Or spread it on wheat toast and top with crumbled bacon.

PREP: *5 minutes, plus 1 hour chilling*	COOK: *none*	COOL: *none*

3 cups bagged grated mild white Cheddar cheese (about 12 ounces)

1 cup bagged grated sharp Cheddar cheese (about 4 ounces)

4 ounces processed cheese, such as Velveeta, grated (see Note)

2 cups mayonnaise, preferably Hellmann's

½ cup drained diced pimientos

¼ cup minced green onion (light and dark green parts)

¼ cup chopped pecans, toasted (see page 79; optional)

1. In a large bowl, combine the Cheddar cheeses, Velveeta, mayonnaise, pimientos, green onion, and pecans (if using). Stir gently until well mixed. Cover and chill for 1 hour before serving.

2. Store in a covered container in the refrigerator for up to 4 days.

Makes about 5 cups; 8 to 10 servings

NOTE: *Grating processed cheese can be challenging because it's so soft. Freeze it just until firm, about 1 hour, to make it easier to grate.*

GRILLED HAVARTI, TOMATO & BASIL SANDWICHES

When the tomato and basil plants in the garden are bursting with fruit and fragrance, I like to combine them with my favorite kind of cheese, Havarti, in these warm grilled sandwiches. They're easy to customize if your family doesn't share my passion for height-of-summer tomatoes and basil, but I highly recommend the Havarti, which I prefer for grilled cheese because it melts so beautifully.

PREP: *10 minutes*	COOK: *about 5 minutes*	COOL: *none*

½ cup mayonnaise, preferably Hellmann's
8 slices French bread or country loaf
8 slices Havarti cheese

1 vine-ripened tomato (see Tip), cut into 8 thin slices
Leaves from 1 small bunch of basil, torn

1. Spread the mayonnaise on both sides of each slice of bread. On each of 4 slices of bread, layer 1 slice of cheese, 2 tomato slices, a scattering of basil leaves, and another slice of cheese. Place the remaining bread slices on top of each.

2. Heat a large skillet over medium-high heat until hot. Toast the sandwiches until nicely browned on both sides and the cheese is melted, 4 to 6 minutes, flipping the sandwiches about halfway through cooking. Reduce the heat to medium if the sandwiches are browning too quickly.

3. Slice each sandwich in half and serve immediately.

Makes 4 servings

TIP: *If you grow your own tomatoes or buy them truly ripe from a farmers' market, store them at room temperature for only a day or two, then move them to the refrigerator. Supermarket tomatoes are usually picked before they are fully ripe, so they're often best if left on the countertop until they fully ripen; then transfer them to the refrigerator. For best flavor, let chilled tomatoes come to room temperature before eating.*

EGG SALAD SANDWICHES

*When Chip was a kid his mom used to pack egg salad sandwiches in his lunch box.
He liked them so much that he didn't even care when the other kids made fun of the smell.
When we were first married I probably made egg salad every week because it was easy
and inexpensive, and because Chip loved it. Even though we were broke, when I served
egg salad on toasted wheat bread garnished with fresh cracked pepper and dill, it looked
sort of fancy and made Chip so happy that I felt like the richest girl in the world. Now
thanks to our chickens I always have plenty of eggs available for this classic salad that
is great for lunch and never goes out of style.*

PREP: *15 minutes, plus 2 hours chilling*	COOK: *20 minutes*	COOL: *30 minutes*

8 large eggs
1 tablespoon distilled white vinegar
Kosher salt
¼ cup mayonnaise, preferably Hellmann's
¼ cup chopped dill pickle
1 tablespoon grated onion

1 tablespoon yellow mustard
1 teaspoon freshly ground black pepper
8 slices soft wheat bread
4 leaves butter lettuce
2 vine-ripened tomatoes, cut into ¼-inch-thick
   slices

1. Place the eggs in a single layer in a medium saucepan and cover with water by 2 inches. Add the vinegar and a pinch of salt. Bring the water to a boil, cover the pan, and turn off the heat. Let stand for 10 minutes. Meanwhile, set up a large bowl of ice water. Drain the eggs and immediately transfer them to the ice water. Let stand until completely cool.

2. In a medium bowl, whisk together the mayonnaise, pickle, onion, mustard, 1½ teaspoons salt, and the pepper. Peel and chop the eggs and add them to the bowl. Stir gently until well blended.

3. Cover and chill in the refrigerator for at least 2 hours and up to 2 days.

4. Make sandwiches using the bread, butter lettuce leaves, and tomato slices. Serve.

Makes 4 servings

SWEET PEPPER & PANCETTA FRITTATA

It's no secret that we love to eat eggs, which I consider a perfect food, so I'm always looking for new ways to serve them. This is one I tend to prepare more often for my friends or mom than for the kids, but the recipe is totally adaptable and the veggies can easily be left out or more can be added if you prefer. For an afternoon lunch with the ladies, this hits all the marks: It's quick to prepare, delicious, and beautiful.

PREP: *15 minutes*	**COOK**: *under 30 minutes*	**COOL**: *none*

8 ounces pancetta, finely chopped

1 tablespoon salted butter (if needed)

2 red, yellow, and/or orange bell peppers, cut into ½-inch dice

8 large eggs

¼ cup heavy cream

2 teaspoons fresh thyme leaves or 1 teaspoon dried

Kosher salt and freshly ground black pepper

4 ounces Gruyère cheese, grated (about 1 cup)

½ cup crumbled feta cheese (about 2 ounces)

2 cups baby arugula (about 2 ounces)

2 teaspoons extra virgin olive oil

1. Preheat the oven to 375°F. Line a large bowl with paper towels and set aside.

2. In a 10-inch nonstick ovenproof skillet or well-seasoned cast-iron skillet, cook the pancetta over medium-high heat until browned and crisp, about 4 minutes, stirring occasionally. If there is little to no fat left in the pan, add the butter and heat until melted. Add the bell peppers and cook until tender, about 4 minutes, stirring often. Scrape the mixture into the lined bowl to drain off the extra grease.

3. Wipe out the skillet and place it over medium-low heat. Return the pancetta and pepper mixture to the skillet.

4. In a medium bowl, vigorously whisk the eggs, cream, thyme, 1 teaspoon salt, and ½ teaspoon pepper until well combined. Stir in the Gruyère.

5. Pour the egg mixture evenly into the skillet. Gently shake the pan from time to time to ensure the eggs are not sticking or scorching on the bottom, and when the edges of the frittata are firm, lift them up with a spatula and gently tilt the pan so that the uncooked egg can run underneath. Cook until the eggs are set and golden on the bottom and sides, about 3 minutes.

6. Transfer to the oven to bake until the eggs are nearly set but still moist on top, about 10 minutes. Remove the pan from the oven and crumble the feta cheese on top of the frittata.

7. Turn the broiler to high. Place the pan under the broiler until the eggs are just set and the cheese is soft, warm, and browned in a few spots, about 3 minutes.

8. In a medium bowl, toss the arugula with the oil and season to taste with salt and pepper. Cut the frittata into wedges, top with the arugula, and serve warm.

9. Store leftovers in a covered container in the refrigerator for up to 2 days.

Makes 4 to 6 servings

CHAPTER 3

Soups & Salads

SOUPS & SALADS

I think of soups and salads as two sides of the same coin. Both are typically made from fresh, natural ingredients that are transformed into something greater than the sum of their parts. And both are the answer to a particular aspect of our family's food preferences. For Chip, who really prefers hot food to cold, a bowl of soup is the equivalent of a warm hug. And to me, that same bowl conjures up a sense of contentment and just an overall feeling of coziness. I naturally gravitate toward comfort foods, and perhaps it's because of the almost indefinable sense of nostalgia that they can give us. When I put a big pot of tortilla soup on the table with all of its toppings and watch the kids dig in, I get a flash of my own childhood, and how glad I was when my mom served one of my favorite meals.

For sure it's never been just about the soup; it's also about whatever accompanies it. For instance, I like to serve beef stew with hot cornbread, and my kids know and love that New Year's Eve means chicken and wild rice soup and warm dinner rolls with plenty of butter and honey. What this is not about is complicating an easy meal with something else homemade. In fact, a good loaf of crusty country bread from the market is my go-to on many soup-for-dinner nights. It's simply about adding that little something extra that makes the meal feel thoughtful.

And on the other side of that coin is how happy it makes me to walk into my garden, pick whatever is ripe, toss it together with a few kitchen staples, and create a salad that is beautiful and delicious—both to our palates and for our bodies. Even if I'm grabbing fresh vegetables from the market rather than the backyard, it's still infinitely satisfying that it requires a little chopping and tossing but not much else. I used to feel like I was mostly winging it when it came to salads, but over the years I've realized that I basically just follow a few simple formulas and swap ingredients in or out depending on what's in season.

Generally my favorite salads are greens and veggies with a few additions that I always have on hand in my pantry or fridge: nuts, cheese, fruit (dried, canned, or fresh—all work well), and a great store-bought or homemade vinaigrette. These are the basic building blocks for the salads I share on the following pages. You can use them as they're written or simply as jumping-off points for creating a few great salad formulas of your own. With a bit of inspiration, you can always throw something fresh and nutritious together in no time at all.

TORTILLA SOUP

The nourishing broth at the base of this soup is mild enough that it's agreeable to any palate—it's the toppings that dress it up and make it unique. Everyone gets to top their own, which is the best way I know how to make sure everyone is happy. I like the texture and heartiness that the seasoned rice contributes. This soup is very easy to make— the most time-consuming part is prepping the garnishes—which is a good place to let the kids jump in and help.

PREP: *15 minutes*	**COOK:** *30 minutes*	**COOL:** *none*

Three 32-ounce cans chicken broth or 12 cups Homemade Chicken Broth (page 216)

1 vine-ripened tomato, cut into ½-inch dice

One 15.25-ounce can corn kernels, drained

¼ cup finely chopped red onion

½ jalapeño (ribbed and seeded if desired), minced (see Note, page 157)

½ teaspoon kosher salt

½ teaspoon freshly ground black pepper

4 cups shredded meat from 1 store-bought rotisserie chicken or Perfect Roast Chicken (page 203)

One 5.4-ounce pouch Mexican rice mix, or a similar mix

1 teaspoon ground cumin (optional)

½ cup chopped fresh cilantro

1 or 2 Hass avocado(s), pitted, peeled, and cut into ½-inch dice

One 13-ounce bag tortilla chips, crushed

2 cups grated mozzarella cheese (about 8 ounces)

1. In a large soup pot, combine the broth, tomato, corn, onion, jalapeño, salt, and black pepper. Bring to a boil over medium-high heat. Reduce the heat and add the shredded chicken. Simmer until heated through.

2. Stir the rice mix into the soup. Add the cumin (if using) and simmer for 15 minutes to cook the rice and let the flavors meld.

3. Place the cilantro, avocado, crushed tortilla chips, and mozzarella in separate serving dishes. Ladle the soup into bowls and pass the garnishes at the table.

4. Store leftover soup in a covered container in the refrigerator for up to 4 days.

Makes 6 to 8 servings

COUNTRY POTATO SOUP
WITH CRUMBLED BACON

When Chip and the kids are working on the farm, I like to make sure they eat well and are ready for a good day of hard work. That can be as simple as sending them off with a Thermos of this hearty soup, a loaf of good bread, and a few toppings. This soup is easy to make and really satisfying, especially with crispy bacon, fresh thyme, and grated cheese on top—I always use all of them, but everyone can customize it just the way they like it.

PREP: *15 minutes*	COOK: *55 minutes*	COOL: *none*

CRUMBLED BACON

½ pound thick-cut bacon

COUNTRY POTATO SOUP

4 tablespoons (½ stick) salted butter

6 garlic cloves, minced

1 medium white onion, cut into ½-inch dice

3 carrots, peeled and cut into ½-inch dice

3 celery stalks, cut into ½-inch dice

½ cup all-purpose flour

6 medium-large russet potatoes (about 3 pounds), scrubbed, peeled in stripes, and cut into 1-inch cubes

One 48-ounce box chicken broth or 6 cups Homemade Chicken Broth (page 216)

1 teaspoon kosher salt

1 teaspoon freshly ground black pepper

1 bay leaf

2 cups whole milk

1 cup grated yellow and/or white sharp Cheddar cheese (about 4 ounces)

1 teaspoon fresh thyme leaves

1. To make the crumbled bacon: Line a large plate with paper towels.

2. **IF USING THE OVEN**: Preheat the oven to 400°F. Arrange the bacon slices on a baking sheet. Bake until crispy, about 20 minutes. Transfer to the paper towels to drain. Crumble or chop.

IF USING A SKILLET: Cut the bacon strips crosswise into ¼-inch-wide pieces. Place in a large skillet and put the skillet over medium heat. Cook, stirring occasionally, until cooked through, about 10 minutes. Use a slotted spoon to transfer the bacon crumbles to the paper towels.

3. To make the country potato soup: In a large soup pot, melt the butter over medium heat. Add the garlic, onion, carrots, and celery and cook, stirring occasionally, until the vegetables are tender, about 10 minutes.

4. Add the flour and cook, stirring constantly, for 2 minutes. Add the potatoes, chicken broth, salt, pepper, and bay leaf and bring to a boil. Reduce the heat and simmer until the potatoes are tender but still hold their shape, about 15 minutes. Remove and discard the bay leaf. Slowly pour in the milk, stirring constantly. Simmer until the soup is slightly thickened and the potatoes are fully cooked, about 15 minutes.

5. Ladle the soup into bowls and top with Cheddar, thyme, and crumbled bacon.

6. Store leftover soup in a covered container in the refrigerator for up to 3 days. Reheat in the microwave or in a saucepan over medium-low heat.

Makes 6 to 8 servings

ROASTED CAULIFLOWER SOUP

Roasting cauliflower until it is browned brings out its natural sweetness more than when it is simply simmered. It's this step that really makes this creamy soup something special. Garnishing it with thinly sliced prosciutto and toasted pine nuts makes it even better.

PREP: *10 minutes*	**COOK**: *under 1 hour*	**COOL**: *none*

10 cups cauliflower florets (from a roughly 2¾-pound cauliflower)
¼ cup extra virgin olive oil
6 tablespoons salted butter
1 white onion, cut into ½-inch dice
1 garlic clove, minced
1 teaspoon dried thyme
2 pinches dried tarragon
1 teaspoon kosher salt

¾ teaspoon freshly ground black pepper
½ cup dry sherry (optional)
5 cups vegetable broth
1 cup heavy cream
8 ounces sour cream or cream cheese, cut into 2-inch pieces
4 ounces prosciutto, thinly sliced (optional)
½ cup pine nuts, toasted (see page 79)

1. Preheat the oven to 425°F.

2. Spread the cauliflower on a large baking sheet and drizzle with the olive oil. Roast until browned in spots, about 25 minutes. Set aside.

3. In a large soup pot, melt the butter over medium heat. Add the onion, garlic, thyme, tarragon, and salt and pepper and sauté until the onion is tender and translucent, about 7 minutes.

4. Add the sherry (if using) and cook for 1 minute.

5. Stir in the vegetable broth and roasted cauliflower and bring to a gentle boil. Reduce the heat and simmer until the cauliflower is very soft, about 10 minutes.

6. Add the cream and sour cream (or cream cheese). Bring to a simmer over medium heat.

7. Use an immersion blender to blend the soup until smooth. (Alternatively, let cool slightly and, working in batches as necessary, process in a stand blender until smooth, filling the blender no more than half full and removing the little steam vent in the lid.)

8. Ladle into soup bowls. Top each serving with a little prosciutto (if using) and toasted pine nuts. Serve hot.

9. Store leftovers in a covered container in the refrigerator for up to 2 days.

Makes 4 to 6 servings

CHICKEN & WILD RICE SOUP

*I love traditions, especially around the holiday season, and this kid-friendly soup is one
of my favorite food-related ones. I prepare it only on New Year's Eve, and I serve it with
warm rolls drizzled with lots of melted butter and honey. My family loves it and they pounce
on it, since they know this meal comes around only once a year. It's my way of wrapping up
the past year and welcoming in the New Year with the people that I love most.*

PREP: *15 minutes*	**COOK**: *50 minutes*	**COOL**: *none*

¾ cup all-purpose flour

1¾ teaspoons kosher salt

1¾ teaspoons freshly ground black pepper

2½ pounds boneless, skinless chicken breasts,
cut into ½-inch pieces

4 tablespoons (½ stick) salted butter

½ cup diced (¼-inch) white onion

½ cup diced (¼-inch) celery

1 bay leaf (optional)

8 ounces baby bella mushrooms, trimmed and
cut into ½-inch slices (about 2½ cups)

2 garlic cloves, minced

¼ cup dry white wine (optional)

One 32-ounce box chicken broth or 4 cups
Homemade Chicken Broth (page 216)

Two 8.8-ounce pouches long-grain and wild
rice blend, preferably Uncle Ben's, cooked
according to package directions

1½ cups milk

½ cup heavy cream

¼ cup chopped fresh flat-leaf parsley, for
garnish (optional)

1. In a large bowl, whisk together the flour and 1¼ teaspoons each of the salt and pepper. Add the
chicken and gently toss to thoroughly coat the pieces in the seasoned flour. Remove the chicken
from the flour, shaking off the excess, and set it aside. Discard any remaining flour.

2. In a large soup pot, heat the butter over medium-high heat until melted. Add the onion, celery,
and bay leaf (if using) and sauté until the vegetables are tender, about 5 minutes.

3. Add the mushrooms and sauté until they give up most of their liquid and are lightly browned,
about 5 minutes. Add the garlic and sauté until aromatic and lightly browned, about 30 seconds.

4. Add the chicken and cook, stirring occasionally, until lightly browned, about 3 minutes (it does
not need to be cooked through).

5. Add the wine (if using) and cook until it is almost entirely evaporated, about 1 minute. Stir in
the broth and bring to a simmer. Reduce the heat and simmer for 10 minutes.

6. Stir in the cooked rice, milk, and cream. Simmer, stirring occasionally, until the flavors come
together, about 20 minutes. Season with the remaining ½ teaspoon each salt and pepper. Remove
and discard the bay leaf. Serve hot, garnished with parsley if desired.

Makes 8 servings

TOMATO BASIL SOUP

WITH GRILLED CHEESE STRIPS

On nights when I just want or need to keep it simple, bowls of rich tomato soup beside some good old-fashioned grilled cheese is a favorite go-to. It's definitely one of the dinners Emmie requests most often. The kids love to have such a delicious "dip" for their grilled cheese slices. And who am I kidding? Chip and I pretty much feel the same way. I don't think we'll ever outgrow this classic and I'm grateful for that.

PREP: *10 minutes*	COOK: *under 25 minutes*	COOL: *none*

TOMATO BASIL SOUP

1 tablespoon extra virgin olive oil, plus more for serving

3 small garlic cloves, minced

Four 14.5-ounce cans diced fire-roasted tomatoes

2 to 3 cups store-bought chicken broth or Homemade Chicken Broth (page 216), as needed

1 teaspoon kosher salt

½ teaspoon freshly ground black pepper

1 cup heavy cream

6 basil leaves, stems removed, plus sliced basil for serving

GRILLED CHEESE STRIPS

⅓ cup mayonnaise, preferably Hellmann's

8 thin slices white bread

4 deli slices Havarti cheese

4 deli slices white Cheddar cheese

1. To make the tomato basil soup: In a large soup pot, heat the olive oil and garlic together over medium-low heat until the garlic begins to brown, about 4 minutes. Add the tomatoes and 2 cups chicken broth. Increase the heat to medium and bring to a gentle boil. Reduce the heat to low. Add the salt and pepper and slowly pour in the cream, stirring constantly. Add more broth if a looser soup is desired. Drop in the basil leaves and stir.

2. Use an immersion blender to puree the soup until smooth. (Alternatively, let cool slightly and, working in batches as necessary, process in a stand blender until smooth, filling the blender no more than half full and removing the little steam vent in the top of the lid.)

3. Meanwhile, make the grilled cheese strips: Thinly spread the mayonnaise on both sides of each slice of bread. On each of 4 slices of bread, place a slice of Havarti and a slice of Cheddar. Place the remaining bread slices on top to make 4 sandwiches.

4. Heat a large cast-iron skillet over medium-high heat until hot. Toast the sandwiches until golden brown on the bottom, 3 to 4 minutes. Flip the sandwiches and toast until browned on the other side, 2 to 3 minutes. Slice each sandwich into four strips.

5. Ladle the soup into bowls. Drizzle some olive oil on top and scatter over some sliced basil. Serve with grilled cheese strips.

Makes 6 servings

SAUSAGE & KALE SOUP

I am thankful that our family is together most nights for dinner, but some evenings there's just no getting around the fact that one or more of us will be coming or going during supper hour. Sports practices, school meetings, and the occasional late work night mean that every now and then I need to prepare something that can accommodate and nourish our family streaming in and eating in shifts. It's also important that it be hearty so that it fills them up, and bonus points for beauty—this soup is all of that. It can stay on the stove for the evening so everyone can grab a bowl as they pass through. Sometimes I leave the kale out and stir it into individual bowls, or you can just stir a handful into the pot each time you serve more. From the first person who eats to the last, everyone always loves this soup.

PREP: *10 minutes*	COOK: *about 1 hour*	COOL: *none*

1 tablespoon vegetable oil

One 14-ounce package smoked sausage, such as Hillshire Farm, cut into ½-inch-thick slices

8 tablespoons (1 stick) salted butter

1 large white onion, cut into ½-inch dice

1 pound red new potatoes, cut into ½-inch dice

4 celery stalks, cut into ½-inch dice

2 carrots, peeled and cut into ½-inch dice

¼ cup all-purpose flour

Two 32-ounce boxes vegetable or chicken broth or 8 cups Homemade Chicken Broth (page 216)

Kosher salt

1 teaspoon freshly ground black pepper

1 pound baby kale (about 16 cups)

1. In a large soup pot, heat the vegetable oil over medium-high heat until hot but not smoking. Add the sausage and fry, stirring occasionally, until browned, 5 to 7 minutes. Use a slotted spoon or tongs to transfer the sausage to a medium bowl and set aside.

2. Add the butter to the pot and melt over medium heat. Add the onion, potatoes, celery, and carrots and cook, stirring occasionally, until the onion is translucent and the vegetables are slightly softened, about 10 minutes. Stir in the flour and cook, stirring constantly, for 1 minute.

3. Add the broth, sausage, salt to taste, and the pepper. Increase the heat to medium-high and bring to a boil. Reduce the heat and simmer until the vegetables are tender and the flavors are combined, about 30 minutes.

4. Stir in the kale and simmer until wilted, about 5 minutes. Ladle the soup into bowls. Serve hot.

5. The soup is best served soon after the kale is added. Store leftovers in a covered container for up to 2 days.

Makes 8 to 10 servings

FROM THE KITCHEN OF MAGNOLIA TABLE WACO, TX.

WHITE CHEDDAR BISQUE

Serve this rich bisque with thick slices of crusty bread, such as warm ciabatta or a baguette. I like to put out a couple of shallow dishes of really good olive oil on the table to dip the bread in. I also like to top the bisque with crème fraîche, which is creamier, thicker, and less tangy than sour cream. The bacon and chives on top add a bit of crunchy texture to this velvety bisque.

PREP: *15 minutes*	COOK: *20 minutes*	COOL: *none*

8 tablespoons (1 stick) unsalted butter

1 medium white onion, cut into ¼-inch dice

3 celery stalks, cut into ¼-inch dice

1 thick-cut bacon slice

½ cup all-purpose flour

½ cup dry white wine (optional)

One 32-ounce box chicken broth or 4 cups Homemade Chicken Broth (page 216)

1 pound sharp white Cheddar cheese, grated (about 4 cups)

1 cup heavy cream

½ teaspoon kosher salt or to taste

1 teaspoon ground white pepper or to taste

½ cup crème fraîche

Crumbled Bacon (see page 103; optional)

¼ cup minced chives, for garnish

1. In a large soup pot, melt the butter over medium heat. Add the onion, celery, and bacon slice and cook until the onion is tender and translucent, about 6 minutes.

2. Add the flour and cook, stirring constantly, for 2 minutes.

3. Stir in the wine (if using) or a little of the chicken broth and use a spoon to scrape up the bits on the bottom of the pan.

4. Add the broth and bring to a boil. Reduce the heat and when the broth stops bubbling, stir in the Cheddar until well combined. Slowly add the cream, stirring constantly. Add the salt and white pepper.

5. When the cheese has melted and the soup is fully combined, remove and discard the bacon slice. Use an immersion blender to blend the soup until smooth and velvety. (Alternatively, let cool slightly and, working in batches as necessary, process in a stand blender until smooth, filling the blender no more than half full and removing the little steam vent from the lid.)

6. Ladle into bowls or mugs and top each serving with a spoonful of crème fraîche, a scattering of crumbled bacon (if using), and a pinch of fresh chives. Serve hot.

7. Store leftovers in a covered container in the refrigerator for up to 2 days.

Makes 4 to 6 servings

AUTUMN BUTTERNUT SQUASH SOUP

When I think of the flavors of autumn, this is the first soup I consider making. Creamy and perfectly seasonal thanks to sweet butternut squash and a generous dose of nutmeg, a bowl of this deliciousness warms you up from head to toe.

PREP: *15 minutes*	COOK: *35 minutes*	COOL: *none*

8 tablespoons (1 stick) salted butter

1 garlic clove, minced

1 small white onion, cut into ¼-inch dice

2½ pounds peeled butternut squash, cut into ½-inch chunks

One 32-ounce box chicken broth or 4 cups Homemade Chicken Broth (page 216)

1 teaspoon ground nutmeg

1 teaspoon kosher salt, or as needed

1 teaspoon ground white pepper

½ to 1 cup heavy cream, plus about 3 tablespoons (optional) for garnish

Toasted Pepitas (page 114; optional)

1. In a large soup pot, melt the butter over medium heat. Add the garlic, onion, and squash and sauté until the onion is translucent and tender, about 10 minutes.

2. Add the broth, nutmeg, salt, and white pepper. Increase the heat to medium-high and bring to a rolling boil. Reduce the heat and simmer until the squash is very tender, about 25 minutes.

3. Stir in as much cream as desired.

4. Use an immersion blender to blend the soup until it is smooth and velvety. (Alternatively, let cool slightly and, working in batches as necessary, process in a stand blender until smooth, filling the blender no more than half full and removing the little steam vent in the lid.)

5. Ladle into bowls and top each with, as desired, a drizzle of heavy cream and/or toasted pepitas.

Makes 6 servings

TOASTED PEPITAS

These are the ideal garnish for any kind of squash or pumpkin soup, and they add excellent flavor and crunch to salads.

PREP: *under 5 minutes*	COOK: *under 5 minutes*	COOL: *30 minutes*

2 tablespoons salted butter
1 cup raw pepitas (hulled pumpkin seeds)
Pinch of ground nutmeg

Pinch of cayenne pepper
Pinch of kosher salt

1. In a large cast-iron skillet, melt the butter over medium heat. Add the pepitas, nutmeg, cayenne, and salt and cook, stirring frequently, until the pepitas are lightly browned and aromatic, 3 to 4 minutes. Transfer to a plate to cool.

2. Store in an airtight container at room temperature for up to 5 days.

Makes about 1 cup

BRUSSELS SPROUTS SALAD

Shredded Brussels sprouts, fresh blueberries, toasted almonds, and poppy seeds are an unexpectedly delicious combination that's also super healthy. The sweetness of the berries and vinaigrette pairs perfectly with the earthy, crunchy leaves and almonds. My favorite thing to serve this alongside is my Grilled Raspberry-Chipotle Pork Tenderloin (page 235).

PREP: *15 minutes, plus 1 to 2 hours chilling*	**COOK**: *none*	**COOL**: *none*

2 pounds Brussels sprouts
2 cups blueberries
1 cup sliced almonds, toasted (see page 79)
½ cup extra virgin olive oil
¼ cup rice vinegar

2 teaspoons honey
1 tablespoon poppy seeds
1½ teaspoons kosher salt
1 teaspoon freshly ground black pepper
2 tablespoons minced chives, for garnish

1. Use a sharp knife to shred the sprouts crosswise, stopping about ½ inch from the base (discard the bases).

2. Transfer the sprouts to a large bowl. Add the blueberries and almonds and toss to combine.

3. In a small bowl, whisk together the olive oil, rice vinegar, honey, poppy seeds, salt, and pepper. Pour over the salad and toss until well coated.

4. Cover and refrigerate for at least 1 hour and up to 2 hours. Dust with chives and serve.

Makes 4 to 6 servings

PEACH CAPRESE

When summer is at its height and the peaches are so ripe that you can smell their sweet aroma just by walking by, it's time for this bright salad—a fun twist on the traditional caprese salad of mozzarella, tomatoes, and basil. This version is really lovely, both from a flavor and visual standpoint, and it comes together in minutes. Just be sure to allow some time for everything to get nice and chilled. First things first: Seek out the best mozzarella you can for the salad. If there's a market close to you that makes it fresh, that's fantastic, but very good mozzarella can be found at your local grocery store. For salads, I like the type packed in water best.

PREP: *10 minutes, plus chilling (for the dressing)*	**COOK**: *none*	**COOL**: *none*

½ cup white balsamic vinegar

¼ cup extra virgin olive oil

2 white peaches, chilled

2 yellow peaches, chilled

Two 4-ounce fresh mozzarella balls, preferably water-packed

10 fresh basil leaves, torn

1 teaspoon flaky salt

1 teaspoon freshly ground black pepper

1. In an 8-ounce screw-top jar, combine the vinegar and oil. Screw on the lid and shake well. Refrigerate until well chilled. The dressing can be made ahead and stored in the jar in the refrigerator for up to 1 week.

2. Remove the pits from the peaches and cut them into ½-inch-thick slices or wedges. Drain the mozzarella if necessary and pat it dry. Use a sharp knife to cut it into ¼-inch-thick slices.

3. On a serving platter, decoratively arrange slices of the white peaches, yellow peaches, and mozzarella. Scatter the basil leaves on top, drizzle over the dressing, and sprinkle the flaky salt and pepper on top. Serve at once.

Makes 4 servings

APPLE CIDER SALAD

This salad came about because I wanted something quick and rustic that I could make either from items I grow in my garden or from what is typically in my fridge and pantry. The softness of butter lettuce leaves, bolstered by the strength of radicchio along with the brightness of watermelon radishes, provides a nutritious excuse to eat good-quality Cheddar and my favorite buttered pecans. Watermelon radishes are beautiful when sliced and have a mildly sweet flavor, but you can always use regular radishes in their place here.

PREP: *15 minutes*	**COOK**: *none*	**COOL**: *none*

2 heads butter lettuce
1 head radicchio
8 watermelon or regular radishes, thinly sliced

2 cups crumbled (see Note) or grated white Cheddar cheese (about 8 ounces)
1 cup Buttered Pecans (page 123)
Apple Cider Vinaigrette (recipe follows)

Gently tear the lettuce and radicchio leaves and place them in a large bowl. Add the radishes, Cheddar, and pecans. Add enough dressing to coat the leaves and toss gently. Serve immediately.

Makes 8 to 10 servings

NOTE: *To crumble Cheddar, use the tip of a sharp knife to chip off little pieces. They'll be varying shapes and sizes, which is what you want.*

APPLE CIDER VINAIGRETTE

This fruity vinaigrette is especially good on salads where one or more of the greens or veggies has a bit of bite, like the radicchio in the Apple Cider Salad.

PREP: *2 minutes*	**COOK**: *none*	**COOL**: *none*

1 cup extra virgin olive oil
¼ cup apple cider vinegar
Juice of 1 lemon

1 tablespoon stone-ground mustard
1 teaspoon freshly ground black pepper
½ teaspoon kosher salt

1. In a 16-ounce screw-top jar, combine the oil, vinegar, lemon juice, mustard, pepper, salt, and 3 tablespoons water. Screw on the lid and shake vigorously until well blended.

2. Use at once or store in the refrigerator for up to 1 week.

Makes about 1½ cups

LAYERED ARUGULA SALAD
WITH PEAR VINAIGRETTE

This is a great salad to bring to a potluck. It looks pretty impressive, and since it's not completely dressed with vinaigrette in the bowl, it stays crisp and fresh even if it sits for a little while. I also like to serve this when the main course is soup and I want to dress things up a bit. The salad is particularly beautiful when it's layered as instructed here, but of course you can simply put all the ingredients in a large salad bowl and toss them together just like a regular salad. When pomegranates are unavailable, I use dried cranberries in their place.

PREP: *15 minutes*	**COOK**: *none*	**COOL**: *none*

PEAR VINAIGRETTE

¼ cup pear vinegar

2 tablespoons minced shallot

½ teaspoon kosher salt

2 teaspoons whole-grain Dijon mustard

¼ teaspoon freshly ground black pepper

¼ cup walnut oil

¼ cup grapeseed oil or mild, extra virgin olive oil

ARUGULA SALAD

5 ounces baby arugula (about 5 cups)

2 firm-ripe pears, peeled if desired, cored, and cut into thin wedges

1 cup pomegranate arils (from about 1 pomegranate)

1 cup Buttered Walnuts (page 123)

½ cup coarsely crumbled blue cheese (about 4 ounces)

1. To make the pear vinaigrette: In a medium bowl, whisk together the vinegar, shallot, and salt. Let sit for 5 minutes.

2. Whisk in the mustard and pepper. Whisking constantly, add the oils in a slow, steady stream. Whisk again just before serving. Store in an airtight container in the refrigerator until needed and for up to 4 days.

3. To make the arugula salad: Spread half of the arugula in a medium glass serving bowl (preferably with straight sides, such as a trifle bowl).

4. Arrange half of the pears over the arugula. Sprinkle with half of the pomegranate arils and half of the walnuts.

5. Repeat the layers once more. Scatter the blue cheese over the top.

6. Just before serving, drizzle a few spoonsful of vinaigrette over the salad, just enough to gloss the arugula, and pass the rest at the table.

Makes 4 to 6 servings

BUTTERED WALNUTS OR PECANS

I always have nuts, butter, and brown sugar in my pantry, so I make these all the time, often in a double batch because they store well. That way I always have them on hand even when I've got very little time. These sweet and salty morsels are such a great addition to salads of all kinds that it's possible I put them on just about every salad in this chapter, even the ones that don't call for them. They're even hard to resist on their own; between me and the little nibblers who pass through my kitchen, only half of these may even make it to be set aside for salads. You may want to hide these from your crew until they've arrived safely on the salad.

PREP: *under 5 minutes*	**COOK**: *about 5 minutes*	**COOL**: *30 minutes*

2 tablespoons salted butter
¼ cup lightly packed light brown sugar

¼ teaspoon cayenne pepper, or to taste (optional)
1 cup walnut or pecan halves

1. In a small skillet, melt the butter over medium heat. Add the brown sugar and cayenne (if using) and stir until well combined.

2. Add the walnuts or pecans and toss to coat. Cook until the nuts are well coated and fragrant, 3 to 5 minutes, stirring frequently.

3. Pour onto a sheet of wax paper and cool to room temperature. Crumble the pieces before sprinkling over a salad.

4. Store in an airtight container at room temperature for up to 4 days.

Makes about 1¼ cups

ROMAINE SALAD

WITH BUTTERMILK RANCH DRESSING
& SKILLET CROUTONS

A salad of crisp romaine and vegetables becomes the salad I most often crave when it's accompanied by buttery skillet croutons and tossed with buttermilk ranch dressing. This is my first choice when I serve nearly any dinner—from casseroles to beef tenderloin. It is my classic, straightforward accompaniment.

PREP: *15 minutes*	COOK: *under 10 minutes*	COOL: *none*

SKILLET CROUTONS

1½ tablespoons salted butter

1 tablespoon extra virgin olive oil

¼ loaf day-old crusty bread (about 4 ounces), cut into ¾-inch cubes (about 2½ cups)

¼ teaspoon garlic powder

¼ teaspoon dried herbs, such as herbes de Provence

¼ teaspoon kosher salt

ROMAINE SALAD

2 romaine hearts, washed and dried

1 pint grape, cherry, or other small tomatoes

½ English cucumber, thinly sliced

3 or 4 radishes, shaved or thinly sliced

¼ cup to ½ cup Buttermilk Ranch Dressing (page 126)

Kosher salt and freshly ground black pepper

Crumbled Bacon (see page 103; optional)

1. To make the skillet croutons: Line a plate with paper towels and set aside.

2. In a large skillet, heat the butter and oil over medium-low heat. When the butter has melted, add the bread cubes and the garlic powder, dried herbs, and salt. Toss to evenly coat the bread in butter, oil, and seasonings. Cook, stirring constantly, until evenly browned, 3 to 4 minutes. Transfer to the paper towels.

3. To make the romaine salad: Tear or cut the romaine into bite-size pieces and place them in a large bowl. Add the tomatoes, cucumber, radishes, and as many croutons as desired and toss to evenly distribute the ingredients. (Store leftover croutons in an airtight container at room temperature for up to 1 week.)

4. Pour over about ¼ cup dressing, season with salt and pepper, and toss to coat. Taste and add more dressing or seasoning if desired.

5. Scatter crumbled bacon (if using) on top and serve.

Makes 6 servings

BUTTERMILK RANCH DRESSING

Good buttermilk ranch dressing is truly one of my favorite things in the world, and not just on salad. I love it as a dip for raw veggies or drizzled on steamed ones like broccoli or cauliflower. Of course you can buy it, but nothing can compare to what you can make at home using real garlic and fresh herbs.

PREP: *10 minutes*	**COOK**: *none*	**COOL**: *none*

1 cup buttermilk
1 cup mayonnaise, preferably Hellmann's
¾ cup sour cream
Juice of ½ to 1 lemon, or as needed
4 garlic cloves, minced
2 teaspoons minced fresh parsley

1 teaspoon minced fresh dill
½ teaspoon minced chives
⅛ teaspoon cayenne pepper (optional)
½ teaspoon kosher salt
½ teaspoon freshly ground black pepper

1. In a medium bowl, combine the ingredients and whisk until smooth. Taste and add more lemon juice if needed.

2. Transfer to a covered container and store in the refrigerator for up to 1 week.

Makes about 3 cups

JO'S QUICK TABLE SALAD

This salad is all about getting great flavors together in as little time as possible. It's a perfect blend of sweet, salty, tangy, and tart. I usually have buttered pecans ready and waiting in my pantry, so this salad makes an appearance on our table almost every week. When strawberries are in season, I use them in place of the dried cherries. If I don't have the vinaigrette already made, I use a good-quality bottled dressing such as Briannas Blush Wine Vinaigrette (it's the one with the strawberry on the label).

PREP: *5 minutes*	COOK: *none*	COOL: *none*

One 5-ounce package spring greens
One 15-ounce can syrup-packed mandarin oranges, drained
½ cup dried cherries
½ cup crumbled feta cheese
½ cup Buttered Pecans (page 123)
Red Wine Vinaigrette (recipe follows)

Place the greens in a large bowl. Scatter the oranges, cherries, feta, and pecans on top. Drizzle over just enough dressing to moisten the salad and toss gently until well combined and the greens are coated. Serve with additional dressing passed at the table.

Makes 4 to 6 servings

RED WINE VINAIGRETTE

Adding a bit of honey to vinaigrette softens the sharpness of the vinegar, and a dash of Tabasco contributes a little kick of spice; you can certainly leave it out if you prefer.

PREP: *5 minutes*	COOK: *none*	COOL: *none*

¼ cup red wine vinegar
½ cup extra virgin olive oil
2 tablespoons honey
½ teaspoon kosher salt
½ teaspoon freshly ground black pepper
Dash of Tabasco sauce (optional)

1. In an 8-ounce screw-top jar, combine the vinegar, oil, honey, salt, pepper, and Tabasco (if using). Screw on the lid and shake until well mixed.

2. Use at once or store in the refrigerator for up to 5 days. Shake well before using.

Makes about ¾ cup

CHAPTER 4

Appetizers & Starters

APPETIZERS & STARTERS

When entertaining, it's a safe bet to assume that your guests will arrive hungry. Laying out two or three appetizers just before or as they come in is a great way to get the party started and help them take off that sharp edge of hunger. I like to put out trays of vegetables, chips, and Parmesan crisps with dips or platters of bruschetta and seasoned crackers in a few different places where we're entertaining so that people have a reason to move around a bit and can get comfortable in the space and with each other. It's like a moveable feast that is in itself an icebreaker—an easy way for people to get past any introductory small talk and really begin to relax and enjoy themselves. Plus it has the secret advantage of giving me some flexibility. Serving appetizers buys me a few minutes to put the finishing touches on whatever I'm serving for the main course and lets me smooth over whatever timing glitches inevitably pop up when preparing a meal for a crowd.

When deciding what I'm going to put out to start, I don't focus on an overall theme for the evening as much as I depend on tried-and-true recipes that are crowd-pleasers. I'm also quick to go for big, bold flavors. There are never any leftovers when I put out a melty wheel of baked Brie coated with sweet, toasted pecans. There's nothing more Texas than a big bowl of warm queso served with corn chips—and you definitely don't have to live here to appreciate its creamy goodness. The key is to choose two or three appetizers that you find simple to pull together so that they don't add any extra stress to your planning and prep.

Something that often happens when we entertain is that people stay long enough into the night that we end up circling back to any remaining appetizers and finishing them off—long after dessert has come and gone. This is one of my favorite things and makes every bit of added effort more than worthwhile. It also feels like a fitting tribute to the greatness of nights spent with dear friends over really good food. I'm pretty sure that if I went full-on tapas-style and served nothing but a bunch of the recipes from this chapter, everyone would be just as happy as they are when I prepare a full meal.

DEVILED EGGS

I don't know if I've ever met a deviled egg that I didn't like, but this recipe is my favorite by a mile. The tanginess of dill pickle relish mixed into the filling with fresh herbs plus the sweetness of brown sugar–glazed bacon makes these deviled eggs look very pretty and taste so good. They're a unique addition to a weekend or holiday breakfast spread, and thanks to the fact that they can be made up to a full day in advance, they're a great option to offer to bring to any potluck. If you have any filling left over after you fill all the eggs, save it for later to spread on crackers or toast. It's the perfect late-night snack.

PREP: *30 minutes, plus 1 hour chilling*	**COOK**: *20 minutes (about 35 minutes if using bacon)*	**COOL**: *15 minutes (for the eggs)*

12 large eggs
½ pound bacon (optional)
¼ cup packed light brown sugar (optional)
1 tablespoon distilled white vinegar
Kosher salt
½ cup mayonnaise, preferably Hellmann's

2 tablespoons dill relish
1 tablespoon minced fresh dill, plus sprigs for garnish (optional)
1 tablespoon minced chives, plus chopped chives for garnish (optional)
1 teaspoon mustard powder
1 tablespoon sweet paprika (optional)

1. If using the bacon, preheat the oven to 375°F and line a rimmed baking sheet with foil.

2. Spread the brown sugar on a plate. Press both sides of each bacon slice in the brown sugar to coat and arrange the slices on the lined baking sheet. Bake until crispy, 14 to 16 minutes. Let cool on the baking sheet.

3. Meanwhile, place the eggs in a single layer in a large saucepan and cover with water by 2 inches. Add the vinegar (see Tip) and a pinch of salt. Bring the water to a boil, cover the pan, and turn off the heat. Let stand for 10 minutes. Meanwhile, prepare a large bowl of ice water. Drain the eggs and immediately transfer them to the ice water. Let stand until completely cool.

4. Peel the eggs, then rinse and dry them. Slice them in half lengthwise. Gently scoop out the yolks into a large bowl. Set the whites aside.

5. Add the mayonnaise, relish, dill, chives, mustard powder, and ¼ teaspoon salt to the egg yolks. Mix well, mashing the yolks with the back side of a fork. Use a spoon to gently fill the whites with the filling. (Alternatively, transfer the filling to a zip-top plastic bag, snip ½ inch off one corner, and pipe the filling into the egg whites.)

6. Chop the reserved bacon (if using) and generously top the eggs with it. If desired, sprinkle dill and/or chives on top or dust with paprika.

7. Arrange the deviled eggs on a platter, cover lightly, and chill in the refrigerator for at least 1 hour and up to 24 hours before serving.

Makes 24 deviled eggs; 8 to 12 servings

TIP: *Adding vinegar to the boiling water makes it easier to peel the eggs.*

PARTY QUESO

Queso is so deeply ingrained in Texas culture that many a visitor has arrived mildly confused regarding our devotion, only to leave a few days later fully enlightened and bought-in. We really love our queso. Who can blame us? There is something extremely right about this warm, creamy, cheesy sauce, with a slew of fresh tortilla chips for dipping. If you've never had queso, you're in for a treat. If, on the other hand, you're a dyed-in-the-wool Texan who is sure that no queso is better than your mom's queso, I get that—just give our family's recipe a try. Your mom never has to know.

PREP: *10 minutes*	COOK: *under 20 minutes*	COOL: *none*

2 tablespoons salted butter

1 medium white onion, finely diced

1 jalapeño (ribbed and seeded if desired), finely diced (see Note, page 157)

2 pounds processed cheese, such as Velveeta, cut into 2-inch cubes

3 cups heavy cream

One 15-ounce can pinto beans, rinsed well and drained

One 15-ounce can black beans, rinsed well and drained (see Tip)

2 cups diced (¼-inch) vine-ripened tomatoes

½ cup minced fresh cilantro

¼ teaspoon kosher salt

½ teaspoon freshly ground black pepper

Blue corn tortilla chips, for serving

1. In a Dutch oven or other large pot, heat the butter over medium heat until melted. Add the onion and jalapeño and sauté until tender, about 8 minutes. Add the Velveeta and cream and heat over medium heat, whisking occasionally, until the cheese is melted and the mixture is well blended, 5 to 7 minutes.

2. Stir in the beans and tomatoes and cook for 2 minutes. Stir in the cilantro, salt, and black pepper.

3. Transfer to a serving bowl and serve warm with blue corn tortilla chips.

4. Store leftovers in a covered container in the refrigerator for up to 3 days. Reheat in the microwave or on the stovetop over low heat.

Makes 14 cups; 10 to 12 servings

TIP: *Make sure to thoroughly rinse and drain the beans so that they don't muddy the bright color of the queso.*

HERBED CHEDDAR SCONES

Scones might be considered more traditional for breakfast or in the afternoon with tea, but I love to serve warm, savory scones as a starter, sometimes alongside a charcuterie and cheese platter. They're great for parties because you can mix and shape them in advance and then store them unbaked in the refrigerator. Just before your first guests arrive, pop them into the hot oven and you'll have freshly baked scones in under 30 minutes— and a house that smells amazing in the meantime.

PREP: *20 minutes*	COOK: *under 30 minutes*	COOL: *5 minutes*

2 cups all-purpose flour

1 teaspoon baking powder

½ teaspoon kosher salt

¼ teaspoon baking soda

¼ teaspoon freshly ground black pepper

8 tablespoons (1 stick) salted butter, cut into pats and chilled

1 cup bagged grated mixed Cheddar cheese blend (about 4 ounces)

¼ cup finely chopped fresh flat-leaf parsley

¼ cup finely chopped mixed fresh herbs (such as chives, thyme leaves, dill, and/or green onion tops)

⅓ cup heavy cream

2 large eggs

1. Preheat the oven to 400°F. Line a baking sheet with parchment paper.

2. In a large bowl, whisk together the flour, baking powder, salt, baking soda, and pepper.

3. Scatter the butter pats over the flour mixture, toss to coat, and work in with your fingers until the mixture is crumbly.

4. Stir in the Cheddar, parsley, and mixed herbs.

5. In a small bowl, whisk together the cream and eggs. Pour into the flour mixture and stir with a fork to form large clumps of dough.

6. Pour onto a work surface, gather, and knead gently to form a cohesive ball of dough. Flatten to an 8-inch round that is about ½ inch thick.

7. Use a sharp knife or pizza cutter to cut the dough into 8 equal wedges. Place on the prepared baking sheet, spacing them at least 1 inch apart.

8. Bake until golden brown, 20 to 25 minutes. Transfer to a wire rack to cool for at least 5 minutes, then serve warm or at room temperature.

9. Scones are best the day they are made. Store leftovers in an airtight container at room temperature for up to 3 days.

Makes 8 scones

ROASTED ELEPHANT GARLIC BREAD

This recipe takes garlic bread way beyond the ordinary. I start with a softened compound butter made with sweet roasted elephant garlic, kalamata olives, and chives. I am generous with the butter when spreading it on the toasted crusty bread. You can't use too much. No matter how I serve this—whether as part of an appetizer spread or alongside pasta or soup—every slice of it is always devoured.

PREP: *20 minutes*	**COOK**: *1 hour*	**COOL**: *30 minutes*

2 elephant garlic heads (see Tip)
½ pound (2 sticks) salted butter, at room temperature
Kosher salt

1 large loaf crusty French bread or country loaf
One 9.5-ounce jar pitted kalamata olives, drained and coarsely chopped
⅔ cup minced chives

1. Preheat the oven to 350°F.

2. Cut off the top ½ inch of each garlic head. Cut off two squares of foil large enough to entirely enclose one head of garlic and place on a work surface. Place each head of garlic cut side down on a foil square so that it sits flat. Place 1 tablespoon butter and a pinch of salt on the uncut side of each head. Bring up the foil around each head and crimp it to seal the garlic inside. Place the packages on a baking sheet.

3. Roast for 45 minutes. Remove from the oven (but leave the oven on). Let the garlic stand, still wrapped in foil, for 15 minutes. Unwrap and let stand until cool enough to handle.

4. While the garlic is cooling, slice the loaf of bread in half horizontally. Lay the two halves cut side up on a baking sheet and toast in the oven for about 15 minutes or until browned. Switch on the broiler during the last 2 minutes for darker toast.

5. Meanwhile, in a medium bowl, combine the remaining 1 stick plus 6 tablespoons butter, the olives, chives, and salt to taste. Press the garlic out of its skins and into the mixture. Use a fork to combine until well blended.

6. Smear the garlic butter on the cut sides of the toasted bread. Slice into 1-inch-wide pieces and serve immediately.

Makes 6 to 8 servings

TIP: *Elephant garlic is not simply a big version of regular garlic; it actually belongs to a different species and has a much milder flavor than regular garlic.*

BAKED SPINACH ARTICHOKE DIP
WITH GARLIC TOAST

If I had to name a few dishes that epitomize the term "crowd-pleaser," this one would top the list. This warm, creamy dip with spinach and marinated artichoke hearts is best served with crusty garlic-Parmesan focaccia toast.

PREP: *25 minutes*	COOK: *45 minutes*	COOL: *none*

GARLIC TOAST

1 loaf focaccia (about 12 ounces)

8 tablespoons (1 stick) salted butter, melted

2 garlic cloves, minced

4 ounces bagged shredded Parmesan cheese (about 1 cup)

¼ cup minced fresh parsley

BAKED SPINACH ARTICHOKE DIP

One 1-pound bag or box frozen chopped spinach, thawed, or 1 pound fresh baby spinach (about 16 cups)

Two 7.5-ounce jars marinated artichokes, drained

One 8-ounce block cream cheese, at room temperature

1 cup mayonnaise, preferably Hellmann's

6 ounces bagged shredded Parmesan cheese (about 1½ cups; see Note)

6 ounces bagged grated Gouda cheese (about 1½ cups)

3 garlic cloves, minced

¼ teaspoon ground white pepper

2 teaspoons dried dill

½ teaspoon smoked paprika

1. Preheat the oven to 375°F. Line a baking sheet with parchment paper.

2. To make the garlic toast: Split the loaf in half horizontally and place the two halves cut side up on the prepared baking sheet.

3. Stir together the melted butter and garlic and drizzle over the bread.

4. Bake until it begins to brown, about 20 minutes. Sprinkle the Parmesan on top and bake until melted and bubbling, about 5 minutes. Remove from the oven and sprinkle the parsley on top. Cut into triangles or wedges.

5. Meanwhile, prepare the baked spinach artichoke dip:

IF USING THAWED FROZEN SPINACH: Wrap it in a clean kitchen towel and squeeze it tight to extract as much liquid as possible. Set aside.

IF USING FRESH SPINACH: Place it in a large sauté pan with a lid and add 2 tablespoons water. Set the pan over medium-low heat and cook until wilted, using tongs to turn the spinach over as it wilts, moving the uncooked leaves on top to the bottom of the pan to cook them. Cover the pan and steam for 2 minutes. Remove the pan from the heat and drain the spinach in a colander. Let stand until cool enough to handle, then wrap the spinach in a clean kitchen towel and squeeze it tight to extract as much liquid as possible. Finely chop the spinach.

continued . . .

continued from page 139

6. Place the artichokes in a large bowl and smash them well with a fork, removing any tough leaves. Add the spinach, pulling it apart with your fingers or the fork. Add the cream cheese, mayonnaise, Parmesan, Gouda, garlic, and white pepper and stir well until combined.

7. Transfer the mixture to a pie plate and smooth the top. Sprinkle the dill and paprika on top.

8. Bake until bubbling and hot, about 20 minutes. Turn the broiler to high and broil until the top is nicely browned. This will happen quickly, so watch carefully and do not step away.

9. Serve hot with garlic toasts.

Makes about 5 cups; 8 to 10 servings

NOTE: *For best results and texture in the dip, use shredded rather than grated Parmesan. And I use shredded on the toast as well because I'm already buying it!*

BAKED BRUSCHETTA
WITH TOMATO, BASIL & FONTINA

When I prepare bruschetta for a party, I usually bake them to warm the fresh tomato topping and melt the cheese. Using a variety of brightly colored tomatoes—red, yellow, orange, and brown—results in particularly beautiful bruschetta. Semisoft Fontina, a cow's milk cheese with a mild, buttery flavor, melts really well.

PREP: *15 minutes*	**COOK**: *under 30 minutes*	**COOL**: *none*

1 loaf French bread, cut on the diagonal into 1-inch-thick slices

½ pound (2 sticks) salted butter, melted

2 cups diced (½-inch) colorful vine-ripened tomatoes (see header note)

1 cup white balsamic vinegar

¼ cup extra virgin olive oil

3 garlic cloves, minced

8 ounces Fontina cheese, grated (about 2 cups)

½ cup basil chiffonade, for garnish

1 tablespoon flaky sea salt, for garnish

1. Preheat the oven to 375°F.

2. Spread the bread slices on a baking sheet and brush both sides of each slice with melted butter. Toast in the oven until lightly browned, about 15 minutes (see Tip).

3. Meanwhile, in a medium bowl, combine the tomatoes, vinegar, olive oil, and garlic.

4. Pull the toasts out of the oven (leave it on) and use a fork or slotted spoon to divide the tomato mixture among the toasts, making sure to drain the liquid from the topping before putting it on the bread. Top each with a generous portion of Fontina.

5. Return to the oven and bake until the cheese melts, 8 to 10 minutes.

6. Garnish with the basil and flaky salt and serve.

Makes 6 to 8 servings

TIP: *You can toast the bread slices up to 1 day in advance. Make sure to cool them completely, then transfer them to a zip-top bag and press out all of the air before sealing it to prevent the toasts from softening. Store at room temperature. Don't prepare the topping or top them until ready to serve.*

GUACAMOLE

Guacamole is one half of what is probably my kids' favorite appetizer—the other half being Fresh Tomato Salsa (page 157). I always serve them together, with tortilla chips. The kids like to dip each chip into salsa and then guac, for maximum greatness in every bite. I really don't know where that got started or which of them did it first, but now all of them do it without fail, every time. The guac-and-salsa combination is also great with enchiladas and tacos. When I make guacamole I keep the avocado a little chunky because our family prefers this texture over something smoother. I suggest a range of onion; use as much or as little as you prefer.

PREP: *15 minutes*	**COOK:** *none*	**COOL:** *none*

4 Hass avocados, pitted

1 medium vine-ripened tomato, cut into ¼-inch dice

2 to 3 tablespoons minced red onion, to taste

1 to 1½ jalapeños (ribbed and seeded if desired), minced (see Note, page 157)

¼ cup chopped fresh cilantro

Juice of 1 lime, or more to taste

Kosher salt and freshly ground black pepper

Tortilla chips or sweet potato chips, for serving

1. Spoon the avocados out into a large bowl and discard the peels. Smash the avocados with the back of a fork until they're broken down but still have lots of texture. Add the tomato, onion, jalapeño, cilantro, lime juice, and ¼ teaspoon each of salt and pepper. Use the fork to stir until well combined. Taste and add more lime juice, salt, or pepper as needed.

2. Serve at once with chips.

3. To store, transfer to a container with an airtight lid. Press plastic wrap directly against the surface of the guacamole and cover the container. Store in the refrigerator for up to 6 hours.

Makes about 3 cups

BECK'S CRACKERS

Seasoning saltines using this simple method from my friend Becki makes crisp, buttery crackers that are great with creamy dips such as my Last-Minute Party Dip (page 149). They're also really yummy on top of soups or salads. I like them for parties because they're easy to make and can be prepared in advance. They're the kind of thing that you can put out no matter what else is being served and they're always a huge hit.

PREP: *15 minutes, plus 24 hours standing*	COOK: *none*	COOL: *none*

2 cups vegetable oil

2 tablespoons fresh lemon juice

Two 0.7-ounce envelopes dry Italian dressing mix, such as Good Seasons

1 tablespoon crushed red pepper flakes

1 tablespoon dried dill

One 1-pound box saltine crackers

1. In a large (14- to 16-cup), deep container with a tight-fitting lid (see Tip), combine the oil, lemon juice, Italian dressing mix, pepper flakes, and dill. Whisk to combine.

2. Add the crackers and turn them over a few times to ensure they are fully coated. Let stand for 24 hours, turning the crackers over twice. (They will absorb the oil and the seasonings will adhere to them; they're a little oily but not dripping and very tasty this way.)

3. Store in a covered container at room temperature for up to 1 week.

Makes 12 to 14 servings

TIP: *You need a very big (at least 14 cups), deep container with a tight-fitting lid to make these properly, so that the crackers are not too tightly packed in. You can also use this method to transform ordinary oyster crackers into something pretty amazing.*

LAST-MINUTE PARTY DIP

I came up with this one day in a pinch when I had some friends call unexpectedly to say that they were stopping by soon. I happened to have all these things in my pantry and was both happy and relieved to discover how delicious they were when mixed together. Since that day, I've been glad to have this formula in my back pocket whenever I need it. Be sure to add the freshly ground pepper just before serving.

PREP: *15 minutes*	**COOK**: *none*	**COOL**: *none*

Two 8-ounce blocks ⅓-less-fat cream cheese

1 cup drained oil-packed sun-dried tomatoes, coarsely chopped

One 7.5-ounce jar marinated quartered artichokes, drained and chopped

1 cup minced green onions (light and dark green parts)

1 teaspoon garlic powder

1 teaspoon kosher salt

1 tablespoon freshly ground black pepper, or to taste

Bagel crisps or crackers, for serving

1. In a stand mixer fitted with the paddle attachment, beat together the cream cheese, sun-dried tomatoes, artichokes, green onions, garlic salt, and kosher salt until well combined.

2. Transfer half of the dip to a small serving bowl and top with half of the pepper. Store the remaining dip in the refrigerator and refill the bowl as necessary, topping with additional pepper before serving. Serve with bagel crisps or crackers.

3. Store leftovers in a covered container in the refrigerator for up to 3 days.

Makes about 4 cups

Photographed at left: Baked Brie (page 150) and Last-Minute Party Dip

BAKED BRIE

This heavenly appetizer is so impressive and yet so easy to prepare that it almost feels like cheating. The Brie is gooey straight out of the oven, a consistency that lasts for only a few minutes so it's important to get it from the oven to the serving table quickly. The fact that it doesn't stay melty long has never been a problem because it tends to get devoured really quickly.

PREP: *10 minutes*	**COOK**: *10 to 15 minutes*	**COOL**: *none*

One 1-pound wheel double-cream Brie cheese

4 tablespoons (½ stick) salted butter, at room temperature

½ cup lightly packed light brown sugar

Pinch of kosher salt

1 cup chopped pecans, toasted (see page 79)

6 Granny Smith apples

Juice of ½ lemon

1. Preheat the oven to 350°F.

2. Center the Brie in a pie plate. Set aside.

3. In a stand mixer fitted with the paddle attachment (or in a large bowl with a handheld electric mixer), beat together the butter, brown sugar, salt, and 2 tablespoons water on medium speed until the mixture is paste-like. Add the pecans and beat just until combined. Spread the mixture on top of the Brie; it'll be roughly 1 inch thick.

4. Bake until the Brie looks like its sides are about to give way, 10 to 15 minutes.

5. Meanwhile, core and slice the apples into wedges. In a large bowl, toss the wedges with the lemon juice to prevent browning.

6. Serve the warm Brie immediately with the apple slices.

Makes 8 to 10 servings

SHEET PAN NACHOS

This is a really fun appetizer to prepare and the surest way I know to keep a bunch of hungry people happy and occupied while you finish up whatever you've got cooking in the kitchen. I usually make the seasoned meat as well as measure out everything in advance so I can toss it all together on a baking sheet and have it ready quickly when hunger strikes. I use Texas-based Julio's brand tortilla chips because I love the Tex-Mex seasoning on them. If you can't find Julio's where you are, use your favorite seasoned or salted tortilla chips.

PREP: *15 minutes*	**COOK**: *under 25 minutes*	**COOL**: *none*

½ pound ground beef (80% lean)

1½ teaspoons chili powder, or to taste

½ teaspoon garlic powder

½ teaspoon garlic salt

¼ teaspoon smoked paprika

¼ teaspoon kosher salt, or to taste

¼ teaspoon freshly ground black pepper

10 ounces seasoned tortilla chips, such as Julio's

¾ cup grated Monterey Jack cheese (about 3 ounces)

¾ cup grated sharp Cheddar cheese (about 3 ounces)

1 cup rinsed and drained canned black beans

1 Hass avocado, pitted, peeled, and cut crosswise into ⅛-inch-thick slices

¾ cup sour cream

½ cup sliced black olives

2 green onions (light and dark green parts), thinly sliced

¼ cup minced fresh cilantro

Fresh Tomato Salsa (page 157)

1 lime, cut into wedges

1. Preheat the oven to 350°F. Line a large sheet pan (rimmed baking sheet) with parchment paper or foil.

2. In a medium skillet, brown the ground beef over medium heat until fully cooked, stirring often to break up the meat, 7 to 9 minutes. Pour off any standing liquid. Add the chili powder, garlic powder, garlic salt, paprika, kosher salt, pepper, and 2 tablespoons water and stir to fully combine. Remove from the heat.

3. Spread the chips on the sheet pan. Spoon generous portions of the meat on top, followed by the cheeses and the black beans.

4. Bake until the cheeses are melted and golden, 12 to 15 minutes. Top with the avocado, sour cream, black olives, green onions, and cilantro and serve at once with salsa and lime wedges.

Makes 6 servings

WHITE BEAN HUMMUS

I think people assume that making hummus is a bit of a chore and it's one of those things that you should just buy, but the truth is that it is so easy to make and it comes together in just a few minutes. I love that this version is both delicious right away and gets even better the longer it sits—so you can make it ahead or whip it up in the moment and either way have great results. Serve it with pita chips or fresh vegetables.

PREP: *10 minutes*	**COOK**: *none*	**COOL**: *none*

Two 15-ounce cans Great Northern beans, rinsed well and drained

½ cup pine nuts, toasted (see page 79)

1 to 2 tablespoons fresh lemon juice, to taste

2 tablespoons roasted garlic (see Note)

1 teaspoon garlic salt

1 teaspoon kosher salt

½ cup extra virgin olive oil

¼ cup chopped roasted red peppers, for garnish

2 tablespoons parsley leaves, for garnish

Bean chips, potato chips, or fresh vegetables (see page 154), for serving

1. In a food processor, pulse the beans, half of the pine nuts, the lemon juice, roasted garlic, garlic salt, and salt until blended. With the motor running, slowly drizzle in the oil and process until smooth. Taste and add more lemon juice if desired.

2. Pour the hummus into a small serving bowl. You can serve it at once or cover and chill before serving. Garnish with the roasted red peppers, the remaining pine nuts, and the parsley leaves. Serve with bean chips, potato chips, or fresh vegetables.

3. Store in an airtight container in the refrigerator for up to 4 days.

Makes about 3 cups; 4 to 6 servings

NOTE: *Follow the method for roasting garlic in Roasted Elephant Garlic Bread (page 137) to roast 2 whole heads of garlic. Once they are cool enough to handle, press the garlic out of their skins and into a small dish. Use a fork to mash the garlic into a paste. Store any extra in a covered container in the refrigerator for up to 4 days.*

PREPARING VEGETABLES FOR A CRUDITÉ PLATTER

Fresh vegetables are a beautiful and delicious accompaniment to all kinds of dips. Sliced bell peppers (red, yellow, and orange), snow peas, celery sticks, carrot sticks, cucumber slices, grape tomatoes, and sliced or whole baby radishes are great served raw.

Firmer vegetables, such as asparagus, snap peas, and broccoli and cauliflower florets, should be blanched and shocked in ice water before serving. You don't want to completely cook these, as they should be almost as crisp as when raw. You just want to brighten their color and soften them very slightly to make them easier to enjoy.

To blanch vegetables, first cut them all to approximately the same size. Bring a large pot of salted water to a rolling boil. Prepare a bowl of ice water and set it aside. Place the vegetable in the boiling water and cook for 30 seconds to 2 minutes, depending on the thickness of the vegetable, until it is very slightly softened and its color is very bright. If blanching asparagus, add the stalks first and cook for 30 seconds to 1 minute, depending on thickness, and then add the tips and cook for another 30 seconds to 1 minute.

Use a spider or slotted spoon to immediately transfer the vegetables to the ice water. Let stand until completely cool. Drain the vegetables thoroughly and dry them with a clean kitchen towel before serving.

FRESH TOMATO SALSA

Good salsa is so essential to me that I don't think I've ever served tacos or enchiladas at our home without also making fresh tomato salsa to go with it. To me, it's just such a perfect blend of natural ingredients, most of which are in our garden, so when it's the right season, I pretty much always have exactly what I need to make it. Plus the homemade version tastes so fresh. I also like that I can tailor it to my family's preferences. Someone hates cilantro? Leave it out. Love spice? Add the larger amount of jalapeño and leave in some ribs and seeds. It's a totally forgiving and flexible recipe that comes together in just a few minutes, and can be served right away or stored for a few days.

PREP: *15 minutes*	COOK: *none*	COOL: *none*

¼ red onion, coarsely chopped

1½ pounds vine-ripened tomatoes, cut into large pieces

¼ cup coarsely chopped fresh cilantro

1 or 2 jalapeños (ribbed and seeded if desired; see Note), coarsely chopped

1 garlic clove, chopped (optional)

Juice of ½ lime, or to taste

¼ teaspoon kosher salt, or to taste

Tortilla chips, for serving

1. In a food processor, pulse the onion until finely diced. Add the tomatoes, cilantro, jalapeño(s), and garlic (if using) and pulse until well chopped.

2. Stir in the lime juice and salt.

3. Serve with tortilla chips.

4. Store in an airtight container in the refrigerator for up to 3 days. Stir before serving.

Makes about 4 cups

NOTE: *A chile's heat is not primarily in the seeds, but in the pithy ribs that the seeds are attached to. If you remove only the seeds, a hot chile will still be super spicy; remove the ribs as well if you want to minimize the heat. If you like super spicy salsa, use the larger amount of jalapeño and leave some or all of the ribs.*

CHAPTER 5

Side Dishes

SIDE DISHES

I love to cook dinner, but coming up with full meal plans, including all the sides, can be stressful and exhausting. It's also all too easy to get stuck in a rut, serving the same few things over and over again. To avoid this predicament, I've learned to approach planning dinner the same way I plan interiors. When I design a space, whether it's a full living room or simply setting the table for a dinner party, I think in terms of adding layers of color and texture until the space looks and feels right. I do this same thing with planning a meal. First, I choose the main course, which is what anchors a meal. I imagine it on the plate and then consider what other flavors, colors, and textures the plate needs so that the meal is well balanced. For instance, I'll envision a couple of slices of my favorite meat loaf on the plate and then think about what will best complement it—what comes to mind might be mac and cheese and a fresh green salad. Or if I want to re-create something that reminds me of my childhood, I'll pick fluffy, buttery mashed potatoes and the bright color of green beans amandine. When I make a beef tenderloin, I'm likely to add roasted asparagus with red wine Béarnaise sauce because the green vegetable balances the richness of the meat and both pair so well with the sauce. The bright yellow creamy squash casserole with green chiles is another side that often comes to mind to accompany so many of our favorite entrees.

No matter what I'm serving, and much to the delight of Chip and the kids, I almost always include warm bread and butter with the meal. I can hardly think of a dinner that it doesn't complement and it also guarantees that if not much else on the table thrills one of the kids, they won't go to bed hungry. Sometimes I bake the bread fresh, but more often it's something that I pick up from the bakery or one of the very good types that are sold "half baked" and are kept frozen until needed, and then I finish baking it in the oven just before serving.

Whether or not you approach dinner planning like I do, one thing we can all benefit from is a good selection of straightforward, sure-fire recipes that our own families love, so that we can rotate through them as we need to. The collection in this chapter is also a great resource for when you've offered to bring something to a casual dinner party or potluck. Great side dishes are almost always welcome additions to any gathering, and these recipes will ensure that you go home with an empty serving dish scraped clean.

ROASTED ASPARAGUS
WITH RED WINE BÉARNAISE SAUCE

I love to grow asparagus, but cooking it just right can be challenging—overcooked and it's mushy, undercooked and it's bitter. Roasting asparagus quickly in a hot oven is one of the best ways I know to bring out the maximum amount of flavor while preserving a really nice texture. Serving the roasted asparagus with a rich Béarnaise sauce makes it feel like a restaurant-quality dish. Use a full-bodied red wine or high-quality vinegar in the Béarnaise for the most beautiful color and best flavor. I love this asparagus best with grilled steak or beef tenderloin.

PREP: *20 minutes*	**COOK**: *about 15 minutes*	**COOL**: *none*

ROASTED ASPARAGUS

1 pound asparagus

2 teaspoons olive oil

Kosher salt and freshly ground black pepper

RED WINE BÉARNAISE SAUCE

½ cup fruity, full-bodied red wine, such as Malbec, or good-quality red wine vinegar

3 tablespoons sherry vinegar

1 small shallot, minced (about 2 tablespoons)

2 large egg yolks

8 tablespoons (1 stick) salted butter, melted

1 teaspoon finely chopped fresh tarragon

1 teaspoon finely chopped chives

1. Preheat the oven to 400°F.

2. To prepare the roasted asparagus: If the asparagus is fresh and reasonably thin, peel the lower half of each stalk with a vegetable peeler. Or, if it is thicker, snap off the tough ends. Place the stalks in a single layer on a rimmed baking sheet. Drizzle with the oil and roll to coat. Season to taste with salt and pepper. Set aside.

3. To make the red wine béarnaise sauce: In a small saucepan, bring the wine, sherry vinegar, and shallot to a boil and cook until the mixture reduces to 3 tablespoons, about 2 minutes. Set aside to cool to room temperature.

4. Roast the asparagus until barely tender with a few browned spots and lightly frizzled ends, 8 to 12 minutes, depending on the thickness of the stalks.

5. Meanwhile, to finish the sauce, in a small stainless-steel bowl or the top of a double boiler, combine the egg yolks and the cooled wine mixture. Nest the bowl over a pot of simmering water (the bowl should not touch the water) and whisk until the egg yolks thicken to the consistency of softly whipped cream, 3 to 4 minutes.

6. Whisking constantly, add the melted butter in a slow, steady stream. The sauce will thicken and increase in volume. Whisk in the tarragon and chives. Remove the pan from the heat. Leave the bowl over the water to keep the sauce warm while the asparagus roasts. Béarnaise cannot be cooled and reheated.

7. Serve the asparagus warm topped with some of the sauce and pass the rest at the table.

Makes 4 to 6 servings

BRUSSELS SPROUTS

WITH CRISPY BACON, TOASTED PECANS
& BALSAMIC REDUCTION

Brussels sprouts can be absolutely delicious, but the kids won't get anywhere near them if they're at all overcooked and bitter. But when I serve them this way—roasted until slightly crispy, drizzled with reduced balsamic that tastes both sweet and tangy, and generously topped with toasted seasoned pecans and bacon—they welcome them onto their plates. I like to serve these with roasted or grilled pork or chicken.

PREP: *10 minutes*	COOK: *under 1 hour*	COOL: *none*

1 pound thick-cut bacon
2 pounds Brussels sprouts, trimmed and halved through the stem
2 tablespoons extra virgin olive oil
1 teaspoon kosher salt
½ teaspoon freshly ground black pepper

3 tablespoons unsalted butter
2 cups coarsely chopped pecans
1 tablespoon lightly packed light brown sugar
1 teaspoon garlic salt
Balsamic Reduction (page 166) to taste

1. Preheat the oven to 400°F.

2. Arrange the bacon slices on 1 or 2 separate baking sheets. Bake until crispy, about 20 minutes. Line another baking sheet with paper towels and transfer the bacon to the paper towels to drain. Chop crosswise and set aside.

3. Meanwhile, toss the Brussels sprouts with olive oil, salt, and pepper. Arrange on a rimmed baking sheet cut sides down. Roast until browned and the edges are crisp, about 30 minutes, shaking the pan occasionally.

4. In a large sauté pan or skillet, melt the butter over medium heat. Add the pecans, brown sugar, and garlic salt and cook, stirring frequently, until toasted, about 5 minutes. Remove from the heat and set aside.

5. Transfer the Brussels sprouts to a large serving bowl. Drizzle balsamic reduction over the top and sprinkle with the pecans and bacon.

Makes 6 servings

BALSAMIC REDUCTION

Simmering balsamic vinegar to concentrate it transforms the vinegar into a sweet-tart syrup that adds incredible flavor to anything it touches. Drizzle this reduction on pizza, pasta, cheese, fruit, greens, grilled fish, or pretty much anything you like to eat. Once you have it in the kitchen, you'll think up all sorts of things to do with it—good luck restraining yourself from simply licking it off a spoon!

PREP: *1 minute*	**COOK**: *30 minutes*	**COOL**: *15 minutes*

1 cup balsamic vinegar

1. In a small saucepan, bring the balsamic to a simmer over medium heat. Simmer until reduced to 4 tablespoons, about 30 minutes. Pay attention as the reduction gets closer to the targeted amount, as it can go quickly toward the end and will burn if it gets too low. Remove from the heat and let cool.

2. Store in a tightly covered container at room temperature if using on the same day it's made, or store in the refrigerator for up to 2 weeks. Bring to room temperature before using to make it easier to drizzle.

Makes 4 tablespoons

TIP: *Be sure to turn the kitchen fan on high when simmering the balsamic to catch the sharp vinegar fumes.*

BECKI'S MAC & CHEESE

I love to eat all kinds of food, but in all honesty if you told me I could have only one thing every day for the rest of my life, it would be mac and cheese. I realize this is exactly the choice that many eight-year-olds I know would make, and I'm okay with that. I first had this recipe, which has become my favorite, at my friend Becki's house. Her family has become a part of our own, and she knows just how much I love mac and cheese. It has become a tradition of ours that every time we join her family for dinner at their house, she makes this side for us. It's simple and creamy enough to please all the kids, while the blend of cheeses and optional crispy panko topping makes it feel interesting to adults. Since I started making this recipe for my own family, my favorite things to pair it with are Almond Chicken Tenderloins (page 211) or Meat Loaf (page 259).

PREP: 10 minutes	**COOK**: 45 minutes to 1 hour	**COOL**: 5 minutes

Kosher salt

16 ounces elbow macaroni, with no ridges

1½ cups heavy cream

½ cup milk

8 tablespoons (1 stick) unsalted butter

8 ounces processed cheese, such as Velveeta, cut into 1-inch cubes

8 ounces Gruyère cheese, grated (about 2 cups)

1½ teaspoons mustard powder

½ teaspoon ground nutmeg

1½ teaspoons freshly ground black pepper

8 ounces white Cheddar cheese, grated (about 2 cups)

CRISPY TOPPING (OPTIONAL)

2 tablespoons unsalted butter

1 small garlic clove, minced

3 cups panko bread crumbs

2 pinches of kosher salt

1. Bring a large pot of generously salted water to a boil. Cook the macaroni until al dente according to the package directions. Drain thoroughly and transfer to a large bowl.

2. Meanwhile, position a rack in the top third of the oven and preheat the oven to 350°F.

3. In a small saucepan, combine the cream, milk, and butter and heat over medium-low heat until warm and the butter is melted. Pour over the pasta. Add the Velveeta, Gruyère, mustard powder, nutmeg, pepper, and ½ teaspoon salt and stir until well combined.

4. Pour the pasta into a 9 x 13-inch baking dish and spread evenly. Top with the Cheddar. Bake until the Cheddar is melted, about 25 minutes.

5. Meanwhile, if desired, make the crispy topping: In a large skillet, melt the butter over low heat. Add the garlic and cook until softened, about 1 minute. Add the panko and salt and toss to coat completely with the butter and garlic. Increase the heat to medium-low and toast in the pan, stirring often, until lightly browned, 7 to 8 minutes.

6. Remove the baked mac and cheese from the oven and let stand for 5 minutes. Top with the crispy topping, if using, just before serving.

7. Store leftovers in a covered container for up to 3 days. Reheat in a 300°F oven.

Makes 8 to 10 servings

DUTCH OVEN CABBAGE & BACON

I generally find it very relaxing to spend lots of time in the kitchen cooking, but every now and then, when my schedule is packed, a recipe that I can prep and leave to cook is a gift. This hearty, tasty braised cabbage dish is an excellent example. It takes just a few minutes to slice some cabbage and onion and put them in a pot with a few other really flavorful ingredients and then into a low-heated oven. After that, I don't have to think about it again until about two and a half hours later, when I have a steaming pot of tender cabbage in a buttery, bacony pan sauce. Serve with pan-fried or grilled pork or chicken and cornbread.

PREP: *15 minutes*	**COOK:** *2 hours 30 minutes*	**COOL:** *none*

8 ounces bacon slices

8 tablespoons (1 stick) salted butter, cut into ½-inch cubes

One 3-pound head green cabbage, sliced into thin wedges

1 white onion, halved and cut into ½-inch-thick slices from stem to root

1 Honeycrisp apple, quartered

¼ cup apple cider vinegar

1¼ teaspoons kosher salt

1½ teaspoons freshly ground black pepper

1. Preheat the oven to 300°F.

2. Layer the bacon slices on the bottom of a large Dutch oven. Scatter half of the butter cubes over the bacon.

3. Layer the cabbage and onion in the pot. Push the apple wedges into four "corners" of the Dutch oven so that they are well spaced along the outside of the pot. Scatter the remaining butter on top and sprinkle with the vinegar, salt, and pepper.

4. Cover and bake until the cabbage is tender when pierced with a fork, about 2½ hours. Remove and discard the apple wedges if desired.

5. Serve hot directly from the Dutch oven, leaving the bacon behind.

6. Store leftovers in a covered container in the refrigerator for up to 3 days.

Makes 8 servings

SOUFFLÉED BROCCOLI CASSEROLE

Sometimes I have to talk my kids into eating broccoli, but when it's in this creamy, cheesy casserole, I don't have to say a word. This isn't just kid food, though; we adults also think it's pretty great. This is almost always my go-to when I'm making a roast.

PREP: *15 minutes*	**COOK**: *55 minutes to 1 hour*	**COOL**: *5 minutes*

Vegetable oil spray
Kosher salt
4 broccoli crowns (about 2 pounds), cut into large florets
8 tablespoons (1 stick) salted butter
½ cup all-purpose flour
2 cups heavy cream

1 teaspoon garlic powder
1 teaspoon freshly ground black pepper
½ white onion, grated
1 cup mayonnaise, preferably Hellmann's
6 large eggs
8 ounces Baby Swiss cheese, grated (about 2 cups)

1. Preheat the oven to 375°F. Spray a 9 x 13-inch baking dish with vegetable oil.

2. In a pot with a steamer insert (or in a large covered sauté pan fitted with an expandable steamer basket), bring 2 inches of water and 1 tablespoon salt to a boil. Prepare a large bowl of ice water. Add the broccoli to the steamer insert or basket, cover, and steam until tender, about 10 minutes. Transfer the broccoli to the bowl of ice water until cool. Drain well and coarsely chop the broccoli. Spread it evenly in the prepared baking dish.

3. In a large saucepan, melt the butter over medium heat. Add the flour and cook, stirring constantly, for 1 to 2 minutes to remove the raw taste. Whisk in the cream and continue to whisk to work out the lumps. Add the garlic powder, 1 teaspoon salt, and the pepper and whisk constantly until the sauce thickens.

4. Remove from the heat and stir in the onion and mayonnaise.

5. In a medium bowl, whisk the eggs. Whisking constantly, add about ¼ cup of the hot mixture to the eggs to temper them. Pour the warmed eggs into the saucepan and whisk to combine.

6. Pour the mixture into the prepared baking dish, completely covering the broccoli. Scatter the grated Swiss on top.

7. Bake until the center is set when the dish is gently nudged, 35 to 40 minutes. Let stand for 5 minutes, then serve directly from the dish.

8. The casserole is best served the day it is made. Store leftovers in a covered container in the refrigerator for up to 2 days.

Makes 10 to 12 servings

SCALLOPED POTATOES

When we were dating, Chip would often say that there are about five foods that he really, really loves, and one of them is scalloped potatoes. The sliced potatoes make this a pretty dish, and the cream and cheese mixture tastes like heaven. When we serve steak for dinner and I don't have much time for sides, I'll make mashed potatoes, but anytime I have a few extra minutes, I like to make this one especially for Chip.

PREP: *15 minutes*	**COOK**: *under 1 hour*	**COOL**: *none*

6 tablespoons unsalted butter, plus softened butter for the baking dish

Kosher salt

6 medium-large russet potatoes (about 3 pounds), scrubbed, peeled in stripes, and cut crosswise into ¼-inch-thick slices

6 garlic cloves, minced

2 tablespoons all-purpose flour

2 cups heavy cream

1 cup whole milk

8 ounces Gruyère cheese, grated (about 2 cups)

½ teaspoon freshly ground black pepper

2 tablespoons minced chives, for garnish

1. Preheat the oven to 350°F. Butter a 9 x 13-inch baking dish.

2. Bring a large pot of generously salted water to a rolling boil. Add the potatoes and simmer until just tender but not falling apart, about 8 minutes. Drain thoroughly and set aside.

3. In a medium saucepan, melt the 6 tablespoons butter over medium heat. Add the garlic and sauté over medium-low heat until softened and fragrant, about 30 seconds. Increase the heat to medium, whisk in the flour, and cook, stirring constantly, for 2 to 3 minutes, until lightly browned and fragrant.

4. Whisking constantly, slowly pour in the cream and milk and continue whisking until the sauce is smooth. Add the Gruyère, ¼ teaspoon salt, and the pepper and cook, whisking gently, until the cheese is melted.

5. Arrange the potatoes in the prepared baking dish and pour the sauce over them. Bake until warmed all the way through and lightly browned on top, 25 to 30 minutes. Top with the chives and serve.

6. Store leftovers in an airtight container in the refrigerator for up to 3 days. Reheat in a 300°F oven.

Makes 6 to 8 servings

GREEN BEANS AMANDINE

A garnish of lightly sweetened toasted almonds is one of the best ways I know to get reluctant kids to eat their green beans. These are excellent with the Chicken Spaghetti (page 213) or Fried Chicken with Sticky Poppy Seed Jam (page 223).

PREP: *5 minutes*	**COOK**: *about 10 minutes*	**COOL**: *none*

Kosher salt

1½ pounds green beans, ends snapped

2 tablespoons unsalted butter, melted

3 small garlic cloves, minced

½ cup lightly packed light brown sugar

2½ tablespoons dry sherry or sherry vinegar

1½ teaspoons apple cider vinegar

1 cup sliced almonds, toasted (see page 79)

½ teaspoon freshly ground black pepper

1. Bring a large saucepan of generously salted water to a rolling boil. Add the green beans and cook until al dente, 6 to 8 minutes. Drain thoroughly and set aside.

2. Return the saucepan to medium heat. Melt the butter, then add the garlic and sauté until softened, about 30 seconds. Whisk in the brown sugar, sherry, and cider vinegar. Add the green beans and toss until well coated.

3. Add the almonds, ½ teaspoon salt, and the pepper and toss until well combined. Remove from the heat. Transfer to a serving dish. Serve hot.

4. Store leftovers in a covered container in the refrigerator for up to 3 days.

Makes 4 to 6 servings

CREAMY SQUASH CASSEROLE
WITH GREEN CHILES

This is my version of San Antonio squash casserole, a baked dish of yellow squash, cheese, cream, and chiles that is very popular in Texas. It's often made with sliced yellow squash, but I prefer to grate the squash so that the texture of the finished dish is light and creamy.

PREP: *15 minutes*	COOK: *under 45 minutes*	COOL: *10 minutes*

8 tablespoons (1 stick) salted butter, plus softened butter for the baking dish

1 medium white onion, finely chopped

2 pounds yellow summer squash, coarsely grated

4 large eggs

½ cup heavy cream

1½ teaspoons kosher salt

½ teaspoon freshly ground black pepper

Two 4-ounce cans diced green chiles, undrained

8 ounces processed cheese, such as Velveeta, cut into small cubes

2 cups lightly crushed Ritz crackers (about 3 dozen crackers)

1. Preheat the oven to 350°F. Generously butter a 9 x 13-inch baking dish.

2. In a large skillet, melt 4 tablespoons of the butter over medium-high heat. Add the onion and sauté until it begins to soften, about 4 minutes. Stir in the squash and cook, stirring often, until tender, about 5 minutes. Pour into a fine-mesh sieve and let drain for 5 minutes, pressing with a spoon from time to time to extract as much moisture as possible. Pour into a large bowl.

3. In a medium bowl, vigorously whisk together the eggs, cream, salt, and pepper. Whisk in the chiles and their liquid. Stir in the squash mixture. Stir in the Velveeta. Scrape into the prepared baking dish.

4. Melt the remaining 4 tablespoons butter. In a medium bowl, toss the melted butter with the cracker crumbs. Scatter over the squash mixture.

5. Bake until set and golden brown on top, about 30 minutes. Let stand at least 10 minutes before serving.

6. Store leftovers in a covered container in the refrigerator for up to 3 days.

Makes 12 servings

POTATO GRATIN MINI STACKS

These almost bite-size scalloped potato cakes make for such a great side dish no matter when or how you serve them. We love them with sausage and eggs for breakfast or breakfast-for-dinner nights, just as much as we do with roasted or grilled meat on dinner-for-dinner nights.

PREP: *20 minutes*	**COOK**: *45 to 50 minutes*	**COOL**: *10 minutes*

Vegetable oil spray
2 tablespoons salted butter
3 garlic cloves, minced
⅓ cup heavy cream
¾ teaspoon ground nutmeg
½ teaspoon kosher salt

½ teaspoon freshly ground black pepper
2 pounds small to medium russet potatoes, scrubbed
1 cup grated sharp white Cheddar cheese (about 4 ounces)
1 tablespoon chopped chives, for garnish

1. Preheat the oven to 375°F. Spray twelve 2½-inch muffin cups with vegetable oil.

2. In a small saucepan, melt the butter over medium heat. Add the garlic and cook until tender, about 1 minute. Stir in the cream, nutmeg, salt, and pepper. Remove from the heat.

3. Peel the potatoes and very thinly slice them with a mandoline (see Tip) or sharp chef's knife. Place the slices in a large bowl. Add the cream mixture and gently toss to coat.

4. Stack the potato slices in the prepared cups. Spoon any remaining cream mixture over the potato stacks. Cover the pan with foil.

5. Bake for 30 minutes. Remove the pan from the oven and carefully remove the foil. Top the stacks with the Cheddar. Bake, uncovered, until the cheese is golden brown and the potatoes are fork-tender, 10 to 15 minutes. Let stand for 10 minutes. Sprinkle with chopped chives and serve warm.

6. Store leftover potato stacks in a covered container in the refrigerator for up to 3 days. Reheat in a 300°F oven.

Makes 12 servings

TIP: *A mandoline is a tool that makes quick work of thinly slicing the potatoes, but you don't need one; a sharp chef's knife will do the job as well.*

MASHED POTATOES

My mom would be the first one to tell you that she's not really a cook, but there are a few things that she makes better than anyone I know. My dad has always been a meat-and-potatoes guy, so many years ago she figured out how to make a killer roast, dinner rolls, and mashed potatoes. She taught me this simple recipe and method long before I moved away for college, and I still remember how grateful I was to know it when I first got married.
I can't think of any meal that's not made better by these dreamy mashed potatoes—and thankfully Chip feels the same way. I still make mashed potatoes pretty much exactly how she does, with a couple of exceptions: I always peel the potatoes in "stripes," leaving a little bit of the peel behind, because I like the texture and because it also adds a bit of color; and my mom uses three sticks of butter instead of two.

PREP: *10 minutes*	**COOK**: *under 45 minutes*	**COOL**: *none*

6 large russet potatoes (about 3½ pounds total), scrubbed

Kosher salt

½ pound (2 sticks) salted butter

½ cup milk

1 teaspoon freshly ground black pepper

1. Peel the potatoes, leaving a little skin on each one for texture, if desired (I like to leave about 5 stripes of skin on each potato). Cut the potatoes into 1½-inch chunks.

2. Bring a large pot of generously salted water to a rolling boil. Add the potatoes and simmer until they are very soft, 15 to 20 minutes. Drain thoroughly and return the potatoes to the pot.

3. Meanwhile, in a medium saucepan, heat the butter and milk over medium-low heat just until the butter is melted and the milk is warm.

4. Mash the potatoes using a potato masher, adding the milk/butter mixture in about four parts, mashing as you go, until the potatoes are creamy and well blended but still have a bit of texture.

5. Mash in 1 teaspoon salt and the pepper. Serve hot.

6. Store leftovers in a covered container in the refrigerator for up to 3 days.

Makes 6 to 8 servings

GARLIC & HERB TOMATOES

These were inspired by one particularly productive summer in the garden. All tomato plants seem to produce a lot during the summer, but none so much as cherry tomato plants. I don't know if it's because the tomatoes are pretty tiny, but those plants look like fireworks exploding when they get going. One summer I was frankly overwhelmed, so I just tossed a bunch of them into a pan with a handful of things I had in the kitchen. This ridiculously simple method gives back tenfold in flavor and beauty. They're delicious as a side dish with grilled chicken or fish—I especially recommend them with Cod in Parchment with Lemon & Vegetables (page 237)—or as an appetizer spooned over fresh burrata cheese with toasted baguette slices.

PREP: *10 minutes*	**COOK**: *about 10 minutes*	**COOL**: *none*

2 tablespoons extra virgin olive oil

3 garlic cloves, thinly sliced

5 thyme sprigs

1 pound small red, yellow, and/or orange cherry tomatoes

1 tablespoon coarsely chopped fresh tarragon

¾ teaspoon pink sea salt

Freshly ground black pepper

1. In a large skillet, heat the olive oil, garlic, and thyme over medium-high heat until hot. Add the tomatoes and toss to coat in the olive oil. Cook until the tomatoes' skin splits but they have not burst, 5 to 6 minutes.

2. Sprinkle the tarragon and salt over the tomatoes. Remove the pan from the heat. Crack pepper over the top and serve right out of the skillet.

3. Store leftovers in a covered container in the refrigerator for up to 2 days.

Makes 4 servings

STEAMED ARTICHOKES
WITH GARLIC BUTTER

Artichokes top the list when it comes to my favorite plants to grow in my garden. They are just so beautiful. They begin as tight buds and, if not harvested, end up as brilliant purple flowers. Between those stages is a point at which they are best picked, when they can be steamed until tender and the leaves can be pulled off one by one to be dipped in butter and the soft bits scraped off with your teeth or a fork. I think everything about them is really lovely. And let's be honest, they're also just a really great vehicle for eating butter.

PREP: *15 minutes*	**COOK**: *under 30 minutes*	**COOL**: *none*

4 globe artichokes

1 tablespoon kosher salt

½ pound (2 sticks) unsalted butter, at room temperature

2 tablespoons oil from a jar of sun-dried tomatoes, or extra virgin olive oil (optional)

2 tablespoons fresh lemon juice

3 garlic cloves, minced

1 teaspoon garlic salt

1. Cut off the top ½ inch of the artichokes and use scissors to trim the tops of the outer leaves. Cut off all but ½ inch of the stem from the base.

2. In a wide, deep pot with a steamer insert or fitted with an expandable steamer basket, bring 2 inches of water and the salt to a boil. Add the artichokes to the steamer insert or basket, cover, and steam until a thin, sharp knife easily slides into the base and the leaves are easy to pull out, about 20 minutes.

3. Meanwhile, melt the butter in a small saucepan over low heat or in a glass measuring cup in the microwave. Stir in the oil (if using), lemon juice, garlic, and garlic salt and whisk to combine. Divide among 4 small individual ramekins.

4. Serve 1 artichoke and a ramekin of garlic butter to each person. To eat, pull the artichoke leaves out individually, dip them into the butter, and scrape the leaf against your teeth to remove the soft part. (Place a couple bowls around the table to collect the scraped leaves.) When you are finished with all the leaves, trim away and discard the thinnest leaves and silky choke until you're left with the artichoke heart, which is edible (and some say the very best part).

5. Artichokes are best eaten the day they are cooked.

Makes 4 servings

FRIED GREEN TOMATOES
WITH QUICK RÉMOULADE SAUCE

Green tomatoes are a fact of life for anyone with a garden. When those plants begin to bear a lot of fruit, it can be hard to keep up with all the ripe tomatoes, especially since they need to be eaten fairly soon after they're picked. So gardeners will often harvest some before they've ripened, when they're green, firm, and slightly tart. Slicing and frying them is one of the most popular ways to prepare them in the South and one of the best ways to prepare them anywhere. I love to serve these topped with a quick rémoulade flavored with salty, tangy capers.

PREP: *20 minutes, plus 1 to 24 hours for chilling the rémoulade sauce*	**COOK**: *under 1 hour*	**COOL**: *none*

QUICK RÉMOULADE SAUCE

2 cups mayonnaise, preferably Hellmann's

¼ cup minced chives

1 tablespoon coarsely chopped drained capers

2 teaspoons apple cider vinegar

1½ teaspoons sweet paprika

½ teaspoon garlic salt

FRIED GREEN TOMATOES

3 large eggs, beaten

¾ cup heavy cream

2½ cups fine cornmeal

1 cup all-purpose flour, plus more for testing the oil

2 teaspoons garlic powder

Kosher salt and ground white pepper

Vegetable oil, for shallow-frying

3 large green (unripe) tomatoes, cut into ½-inch-thick slices

1. To make the quick rémoulade sauce: In a medium bowl, stir together the mayonnaise, chives, capers, vinegar, paprika, and garlic salt until well blended. Cover and chill for at least 1 hour and ideally for 24 hours before serving (the sauce tastes better after chilling for a day).

2. To make the fried green tomatoes: In a wide, shallow bowl, whisk together the eggs and cream. In another wide, shallow bowl, whisk together the cornmeal, flour, garlic powder, and ½ teaspoon each of salt and pepper.

3. Line a baking sheet with paper towels. Pour 1 inch oil into a large skillet. Heat the oil over medium-high heat until the oil sizzles when a little flour is sprinkled on top, 20 to 25 minutes.

4. Working with one tomato slice at a time, dredge it in the egg/cream mixture and then the cornmeal mixture, shaking off the excess, and place it in the skillet. Cook until lightly browned on the bottom, 2 to 3 minutes, and flip over. Cook on the other side until lightly browned, 2 to 3 minutes. Transfer to the paper towels to drain. Season with salt and white pepper.

5. Continue to dredge, fry, and season all the tomatoes, adding more oil to the pan as necessary. Make sure that it is hot enough before continuing to fry the tomatoes.

6. Serve hot with the quick rémoulade sauce.

Makes 4 to 6 servings

CREAMED CORN SPOONBREAD

Spoonbread is a moist, savory cornmeal pudding that is basically a staple throughout the South. My simple version includes lots of butter and corn kernels for extra texture and sweetness. Chip loves anything with corn, and one of his favorite things to do is put a couple spoonfuls of this at the bottom of a bowl and ladle a whole lot of chili on top. And I have to agree that this is a pretty fabulous combination. But I think this spoonbread is far too pretty and delicious only to be hidden under chili or beef stew. It's a great side for any type of roast and it's always a favorite at our Thanksgiving dinner.

PREP: *10 minutes*	**COOK**: *30 minutes*	**COOL**: *15 minutes*

8 tablespoons (1 stick) salted butter, plus softened butter for the baking dish

One 14.75-ounce can cream-style corn

One 15-ounce can corn kernels, drained

1 cup sour cream

2 large eggs, lightly beaten

2 tablespoons sugar

½ teaspoon kosher salt

One 8.5-ounce box corn muffin mix, preferably Jiffy

1. Preheat the oven to 350°F. Generously butter a 2½-quart casserole dish.

2. Melt the 8 tablespoons butter and pour it into a large bowl. Add the creamed corn and corn kernels and stir to combine. Stir in the sour cream, eggs, sugar, and salt.

3. Add the cornbread mix and stir only until the dry ingredients are incorporated. Scrape into the prepared dish.

4. Bake until golden on top and nearly set in the center, about 30 minutes. The spoonbread will look slightly undercooked when it's done, but a knife inserted about 2 inches from the center should come out clean. Cool on a wire rack for 15 minutes before serving.

5. Store leftovers in a covered container in the refrigerator for up to 3 days.

Makes 12 servings

CHAPTER 6

Dinner

DINNER

It may sound strange, but preparing dinner is my favorite way to unwind after a busy day at work. I understand that some people might feel exactly the opposite, but it's definitely true for me—as long as the meal planning and grocery shopping have already happened. The key for me is not having to think too hard after a long day. If I can lose myself in the chopping and sautéing, I'm good. If I'm scrambling around trying to get my act together, I end up frustrated, and any joy I usually find in cooking seems to fall away. But when I know exactly what we're having and all the ingredients are already in the fridge, the joy part shows up, and this ritual no longer feels like a chore.

There's something else that happens when I let myself enjoy the process of creating a great meal. My family can tell the difference between when making dinner is a bother and when I'm truly enjoying myself and letting the food that I prepare serve as another way to communicate love to them. The kids genuinely get excited when they see me happily pulling out cutting boards or they smell something sautéing on the stove, especially if they find out I'm making one of their favorites, like chicken and dumplings or sour cream chicken enchiladas. Perhaps the Gaines family just really loves to eat, but we show true emotion over these things. When I was a kid I only ever wanted to go *out* to eat; I was always begging my parents to take us to a restaurant. I find the fact that my kids want to stay home and eat my food a little bewildering but also really sweet. Perhaps it's because I feel so humbled and honored by their enthusiasm that I want to make them as many dinners as possible.

Even if it's a little unusual how much I enjoy this nightly ritual, I think a lot of us would agree that we have to be intentional about creating time to be together in a meaningful way. Whether it's with friends or our immediate family, something important happens around the dinner table. And for many families, dinner is the only part of the day when good time together is actually possible. Having a solid collection of simple and beloved recipes is a really big help toward making dinners together a reality. With that in mind, I've put my family's favorites in this chapter, and wherever it seems especially helpful, I've included sides either as part of the main dish recipe or as a suggestion in the header note. I really believe that our kids will remember these dinnertimes together long after they've grown up—and that alone is worth my time.

SOUR CREAM CHICKEN ENCHILADAS

These enchiladas are a year-round family favorite. I make them at least a couple of times a month, no matter what season it is, because the kids love them so much. And when my friends have babies, I bring this dish to them more than any other. I think everyone likes these enchiladas so much because they are simultaneously comforting and unexpected, both creamy and tangy. I use mozzarella here because it's mild and melts well. If you like a browned top, turn on the broiler for a minute or two after the cheese is completely melted, and watch it carefully because it can scorch easily. Most nights I don't take that extra step, because the kids actually like it better blond. But it's delicious either way. I serve these with Mexican rice and warmed charro beans, and I put the tomato, cilantro, and lime garnishes on the table in individual serving bowls so everyone can choose their own toppings. When I have time I make the Mexican rice from scratch, but in a pinch the packaged Mexican rice mixes at the grocery store make a great stand-in.

PREP: *20 minutes*	COOK: *35 minutes*	COOL: *none*

Vegetable oil spray

Two 10-ounce cans mild green enchilada sauce

One 10.5-ounce can condensed cream of chicken soup

One 8-ounce container sour cream

4 cups shredded meat from 1 store-bought rotisserie chicken or Perfect Roast Chicken (page 203)

One 4-ounce can diced green chiles

One 14-ounce bag grated mozzarella cheese (about 3½ cups)

Ten 10-inch soft flour tortillas (see Note)

1 vine-ripened tomato, cut into ¼-inch dice

½ cup chopped fresh cilantro

1 lime, cut into wedges

Mexican Rice (page 195) or two 5.4-ounce pouches Mexican rice mix, cooked, for serving (I like Knorr)

Canned charro beans or your favorite seasoned beans, warmed, for serving

1. Position an oven rack in the top third of the oven and preheat the oven to 350°F. Spray a 9 x 13 x 3-inch (deep) baking dish with vegetable oil.

2. In a large bowl, whisk together the enchilada sauce, chicken soup, and sour cream. Spread about ½ cup of the sauce in the baking dish. Set aside the remaining sauce.

3. In a medium bowl, combine the chicken and chiles. Toss until well combined. Set aside.

4. Set aside about 2 cups mozzarella for topping the dish. Put the rest in a medium bowl for ease.

5. Sprinkle some mozzarella on a tortilla, then add some of the shredded chicken and chiles. Tightly roll up the tortilla and place it seam side down in the prepared pan. Continue with all of

continued . . .

continued from page 193

the tortillas, chicken, and mozzarella (except for what you've reserved for the top), putting the tortillas into the baking dish as they are filled. Push the others up against one another as necessary so that all the filled tortillas fit in a single layer.

6. Pour the remaining sauce over the filled tortillas. Bake for 20 minutes. Remove from the oven and sprinkle the reserved mozzarella on top. Bake until the cheese is melted, about 15 minutes.

7. Pass the chopped tomatoes, cilantro, and lime wedges at the table. Serve with Mexican rice and warmed charro or other beans.

8. Store leftovers in a covered container in the refrigerator for up to 4 days. Reheat in a 300°F oven.

Makes 6 servings

NOTE: *We're lucky in Waco to have several excellent independent tortillerias where we can buy fresh tortillas, which I use for this dish. If you have a good source for fresh flour tortillas, use those, or just buy the best-quality flour tortillas you can find.*

MEXICAN RICE

I like to serve this rice with enchiladas. If your package of rice suggests that it should be rinsed, pour the rice into a large bowl and cover with tap water by several inches. Swish with your hands a few times, then drain thoroughly in a mesh sieve. Repeat several times, until the water in the bowl stays relatively clear after you swish the rice in it.

PREP: *5 minutes*	**COOK**: *35 minutes*	**COOL**: *10 minutes*

3 tablespoons vegetable oil

1½ cups long-grain white rice, rinsed

1 teaspoon ground cumin

1 white onion, finely chopped

1 garlic clove, minced

One 8-ounce can tomato sauce

2¼ cups store-bought chicken broth, Homemade Chicken Broth (page 216), or water, or as needed

1 teaspoon kosher salt

½ teaspoon freshly ground black pepper

½ cup minced fresh cilantro or parsley, for garnish

1. In a large saucepan, heat the oil over medium heat. Add the rice and sauté, stirring, until lightly browned, about 10 minutes. Stir in the cumin and cook for 30 seconds. Add the onion and garlic and cook, stirring often, until softened, about 5 minutes.

2. Pour the tomato sauce into a 4-cup or larger glass measuring cup. Add enough chicken broth to make 3¼ cups total and stir it into the rice. Add the salt and pepper.

3. Bring to a boil. Stir once, reduce the heat, cover, and simmer for 20 minutes. Remove the pan from the heat without uncovering it. Let stand, covered, for 10 minutes.

4. Fluff the rice with a large fork and sprinkle over the cilantro. Serve.

5. Store leftover rice in a covered container in the refrigerator for up to 3 days. Add a few splashes of water to it before reheating in the microwave or on the stovetop.

Makes 4 to 6 servings

CHICKEN POT PIE

I've been making this simple twist on old-school pot pie for the kiddos since they were toddlers. When Chip and I were first married it was one of the things I experimented with a ton until I got it just right for us. My version is based on a generous amount of chicken stew with a somewhat soupy consistency that makes it perfect for ladling on top of mashed potatoes. My kids love it so much that we have it almost every week during the colder winter months. I'm always happy to make this because it comes together quickly, and especially because it's really fun to prepare something that my family enjoys as thoroughly as they do this dish. It's one of my favorites as well. I use two cans of crescent dough here, but it only requires half of the dough from the second can. I like to form the remaining dough into crescent rolls and bake those off separately so the kids can dip them into the delicious stew.

PREP: *10 minutes*	**COOK**: *about 45 minutes*	**COOL**: *5 minutes*

Vegetable oil spray, for the pan

4 tablespoons (½ stick) salted butter

¼ small white onion, finely chopped (optional)

4 carrots, peeled and cut into ½-inch dice

¼ cup all-purpose flour

Two 32-ounce boxes chicken broth or 8 cups Homemade Chicken Broth (page 216)

Two 22.6-ounce cans condensed cream of chicken soup

4 cups shredded meat from 1 store-bought rotisserie chicken or Perfect Roast Chicken (page 203)

1 cup frozen peas

Kosher salt and freshly ground black pepper

Two 8-ounce tubes refrigerated crescent rolls (see Tip)

Mashed Potatoes (page 181), for serving

1. Preheat the oven to 375°F. Spray a 9 x 13 x 3-inch (deep) baking pan (see Note) with vegetable oil.

2. In a large soup pot or Dutch oven, melt the butter over medium-low heat. Add the onion (if using) and sauté until tender and translucent, 3 to 4 minutes. Add the carrots and cook until slightly softened, about 4 minutes. Stir in the flour and cook for 1 minute, stirring often and scraping the bottom of the pot.

3. Whisk in the chicken broth and continue whisking until the flour is fully incorporated. Stir in the chicken soup. Increase the heat to medium-high and bring to a gentle boil. Simmer for 5 minutes.

4. Remove from the heat and stir in the shredded chicken and frozen peas. Taste and season if necessary with salt and pepper. Pour the mixture into the prepared baking dish.

5. Open one can of crescent dough and unroll the contents onto a surface. Press the perforations together inside each rectangle to make a single rectangle. Set it on top of the stew in the pan, flush against one long side; it will cover about two-thirds of the surface. Open the second can of crescent dough and unroll the contents onto a surface. Set aside half of the dough. Press the

continued . . .

continued from page 197

perforations together inside the two remaining rectangles to make one long rectangle. Place it on the uncovered part of the stew, easing it into the space without overlapping it with the dough that is already there. Tuck the corners and edges in if necessary. The dough should fit pretty neatly on top without needing to crimp the edges. (If desired, form small crescent rolls with the remaining dough and bake them separately.)

6. Bake until the crust is nicely browned and the stew is bubbling around the edges, 15 to 20 minutes. Let stand for 5 minutes.

7. For each serving, place mashed potatoes in the center of a shallow pasta plate and spoon over a generous amount of stew and crust, so that the potatoes are completely covered. Serve.

8. Store leftovers in a covered container in the refrigerator for up to 2 days.

Makes 10 to 12 servings

NOTE: *Your 9 x 13-inch baking pan needs to be at least 3 inches deep to fit all of the stew. If your pan is shallower, pour in the stew until it is about 1 inch from the top of the pan and keep the remaining stew warm on the stovetop.*

TIP: *Instead of the refrigerated crescent rolls, you can use the dough from Jojo's Biscuits (page 18). Leave about 1½ inches between the stew and the top of the pan. Use a 1-ounce scoop or two soup spoons to drop spoonfuls of the biscuit dough to cover the surface of the stew. Bake as instructed above until the topping is browned, 35 to 40 minutes.*

DEDICATION CASSEROLE

A good friend of mine created this wonderful casserole the night before she and her husband hosted a party in honor of their young triplets being dedicated at church. Naturally, she wanted everything to be very easy on the day of the party, so the night before she composed the casserole using already cooked chicken and refrigerated it overnight. Before the party she popped the casserole in the oven long enough to warm it and melt the cheese, without having to worry about the chicken being cooked through. It was a huge hit at the party and she dubbed it Dedication Casserole. It works well as part of a buffet at a party as well as a dish to bring to potlucks. It also makes a great dinner for a crowd and goes well with a green salad.

PREP: *10 minutes*	**COOK**: *40 to 50 minutes*	**COOL**: *none*

Three 6.2-ounce boxes Uncle Ben's Long Grain and Wild Rice Fast Cook

Vegetable oil spray

4 cups shredded meat from 1 store-bought rotisserie chicken or Poached Chicken Breasts (page 85)

One 8-ounce block cream cheese, cut into 1-inch pieces

One 12-ounce jar marinated quartered artichoke hearts, undrained

One 8-ounce can diced water chestnuts, drained

1 tablespoon minced fresh tarragon

1 teaspoon garlic powder

Kosher salt and freshly ground black pepper

4 cups grated sharp yellow Cheddar cheese (about 1 pound)

1. In a soup pot, prepare the rice according to package directions.

2. Meanwhile, if serving right away, preheat the oven to 375°F. Spray a 9 x 13 x 3-inch (deep) baking pan with vegetable oil.

3. Into the cooked rice, mix the shredded chicken, cream cheese, artichokes with their liquid, water chestnuts, half of the tarragon, the garlic powder, and salt and pepper to taste. Stir until well combined.

4. Smooth the mixture into the prepared baking dish. Sprinkle the Cheddar on top. (The casserole can be made up to this point, covered, and refrigerated overnight. Set out at room temperature for 1 hour before baking.)

5. Bake until heated through, 30 to 40 minutes. Sprinkle with the remaining tarragon. Serve right out of the dish.

6. Store leftovers in a covered container in the refrigerator for up to 4 days.

Makes 8 to 10 servings

PERFECT ROAST CHICKEN

It takes me just a few minutes once the kids are in bed for the night to get a chicken ready to roast the next evening. The first thing that I do is rub softened butter directly on the meat and sprinkle salt all over the skin 24 hours in advance for an incredibly juicy chicken with perfectly crispy skin. Then, when it's time to roast, I put halved garlic heads in the same pan so that the flavors and cooking juices of both chicken and garlic can further meld. This is the easiest path I know to the kind of perfect roast chicken that you can usually only get in restaurants. I typically serve it along with mashed potatoes and my Brussels Sprouts with Crispy Bacon, Toasted Pecans & Balsamic Reduction (page 165).

PREP: *15 minutes, plus overnight chilling*	**COOK**: *50 to 60 minutes*	**COOL**: *10 minutes*

3 tablespoons salted butter, at room temperature

Finely grated zest of 1 lemon (reserve the lemon)

½ teaspoon finely chopped thyme leaves

½ teaspoon finely chopped rosemary leaves

½ teaspoon freshly ground black pepper

One 3-pound whole chicken

3 thyme sprigs

2 rosemary sprigs

2 teaspoons kosher salt

2 garlic heads, halved crosswise

Extra virgin olive oil

1. The night before roasting, in a small bowl, mix together the butter, lemon zest, thyme leaves, rosemary leaves, and pepper.

2. Blot the chicken dry with paper towels and place it breast side up on a rimmed baking sheet. Use your fingers to gently loosen the skin and separate it from the meat, making sure not to puncture or tear the skin. Tuck the butter mixture under the skin, press the skin back in place, and rub to spread the butter evenly over the meat.

3. Cut the reserved zested lemon in half and tuck it inside the cavity, along with the thyme and rosemary sprigs. Sprinkle the salt evenly over the top and sides of the chicken. Refrigerate uncovered overnight.

4. Preheat the oven to 450°F.

5. Gently brush away any undissolved salt on the chicken. You can either roast on the baking sheet or in a large cast-iron skillet. If using the baking sheet, blot away any liquid accumulated on it. Position the chicken on the baking sheet or in the skillet so that when the pan goes in the oven, the breast will face the back of the oven and the legs will face forward.

6. Rub the garlic halves all over with olive oil and arrange them cut side down around the chicken.

continued . . .

continued from page 203

7. Roast for 45 minutes, then brush or spoon pan juices over the chicken. Continue roasting until an instant-read thermometer inserted into the thickest part of the thigh (without touching bone) registers 165°F, 5 to 10 minutes longer.

8. If the skin on top is not as browned as you like, remove the chicken from the oven, set the broiler to high, and place the chicken under the broiler until the top skin is browned and sizzling, 1 to 4 minutes. Watch carefully so that it doesn't burn.

9. Let the chicken rest for at least 10 minutes before carving. Serve the halved garlic heads alongside the chicken and let diners squeeze out the roasted garlic.

10. Store leftovers in a covered container in the refrigerator for up to 3 days.

Makes 4 servings

KING RANCH CHICKEN
WITH MEXICAN-STYLE JICAMA SALAD

Every Texan cook I know has his or her own version of this delightfully messy enchilada casserole that includes chicken, beans, chiles, salsa verde, sour cream, corn tortillas, and plenty of melted cheese. The most important part of my own version may actually be what I serve it with: a crunchy jicama salad flavored with lime zest and juice, smoked paprika, cilantro, and diced avocado. The crispness of this salad really complements the cheesy casserole.

PREP: 20 minutes, plus 1 to 4 hours chilling (for the salad)	**COOK**: 45 minutes	**COOL**: 10 minutes

JICAMA SALAD

2¾ pounds jicama, peeled and cut into batons 3 inches long and ¼ inch wide (about 10 cups)

Grated zest of 2 limes

Juice of 4 limes

1 cup minced fresh cilantro leaves

1 teaspoon cayenne pepper

1 teaspoon smoked paprika

2 teaspoons kosher salt

2 Hass avocados, pitted, peeled, and cut into ¼-inch dice

2 teaspoons minced chives, for garnish

KING RANCH CHICKEN

Vegetable oil spray

2 tablespoons extra virgin olive oil

1 large white onion, cut into ¼-inch dice

2 cups store-bought chicken broth or Homemade Chicken Broth (page 216)

One 15-ounce can black beans, rinsed and very well drained

One 10.5-ounce can condensed cream of chicken soup

One 16-ounce jar salsa verde (tomatillo sauce)

One 15-ounce can mild enchilada sauce

One 8-ounce container sour cream

1 tablespoon smoked paprika

1 teaspoon garlic salt

1 teaspoon kosher salt

1 teaspoon freshly ground black pepper

6 cups shredded meat from store-bought rotisserie chicken or Poached Chicken Breasts (page 85)

Two 4-ounce cans fire-roasted diced green chiles

20 corn tortillas, cut into ¾-inch-wide strips

4 cups grated sharp Cheddar cheese (about 1 pound)

2 cups grated Monterey Jack cheese (about 8 ounces)

1. To make the jicama salad: In a large bowl, combine the jicama, lime zest, lime juice, cilantro, cayenne, paprika, salt, and 1 teaspoon water. Toss to combine. Add the avocado and very gently toss. Cover the bowl and chill for at least 1 hour and up to 4 hours before serving.

2. To make the King Ranch chicken: Preheat the oven to 350°F. Spray a 9 x 13 x 3-inch (deep) baking dish with vegetable oil.

3. In a 7-quart soup pot, heat the olive oil over medium heat. Add the onion and sauté until tender, about 6 minutes.

continued . . .

continued from page 207

4. Add the broth, beans, chicken soup, salsa verde, enchilada sauce, sour cream, paprika, garlic salt, kosher salt, and pepper. Stir until well incorporated. Bring to a simmer over medium heat. Stir in the chicken, chiles, tortilla strips, and Cheddar until well combined.

5. Pour into the prepared baking dish and scatter the Monterey Jack on top.

6. Bake until heated through and the Monterey Jack is melted and lightly browned, about 30 minutes. Let stand 10 minutes before serving.

7. Just before serving, top the jicama salad with minced chives. Serve the King Ranch chicken with the jicama salad.

8. Store leftover King Ranch chicken in a covered container in the refrigerator for up to 3 days. Store leftover jicama salad in a covered container in the refrigerator for up to 1 day.

Makes 8 to 10 servings

ALMOND CHICKEN TENDERLOINS

These nuggets are a slightly grown-up version of chicken fingers. I say "slightly" because they're not so sophisticated that my kids don't love them, but they upgrade classic fried chicken fingers enough that adults are sure to enjoy them, too.

PREP: *10 minutes*	**COOK**: *under 20 minutes*	**COOL**: *none*

½ cup almond flour

½ cup all-purpose flour

1 teaspoon granulated garlic or garlic powder

1 teaspoon onion powder

1 teaspoon Italian seasoning

½ teaspoon freshly ground black pepper

1½ pounds chicken tenders

1½ teaspoons kosher salt

8 tablespoons (1 stick) salted butter

4 tablespoons extra virgin olive oil

½ cup sliced almonds

Juice of 1 lemon

3 tablespoons chopped fresh flat-leaf parsley, for garnish

1. On a plate, stir together both flours, the granulated garlic, onion powder, Italian seasoning, and pepper.

2. Season the tenders with the salt, then coat evenly in the flour mixture, pressing to help adhere. Set aside in a single layer.

3. In a large, heavy skillet, heat 2 tablespoons of the butter and 2 tablespoons of the oil over medium-high heat. When sizzling, add half of the tenders in a single layer, taking care to not crowd them in the pan. Cook until golden brown on the bottom, flip once with tongs, and cook the other side until golden brown and the chicken is cooked through, about 3 minutes per side. Watch them carefully because they can scorch easily. Transfer to a serving platter and tent with foil to keep them warm.

4. Wipe out the skillet if any of the flour mixture has scorched.

5. Repeat with 2 tablespoons butter, the remaining 2 tablespoons oil, and the remaining chicken. Transfer to the platter. Wipe out the skillet.

6. Melt the remaining 4 tablespoons butter in the skillet over medium heat. When the butter is foaming, stir in the almonds and cook until golden, stirring often, about 30 seconds. Remove from the heat and add the lemon juice. Pour over the chicken.

7. Sprinkle the parsley over the top and serve warm.

8. Store leftovers in a covered container in the refrigerator for up to 3 days.

Makes 4 to 6 servings

CHICKEN SPAGHETTI

Life is a lot easier when you've got a great go-to recipe for this classic one-pot Southern dinner. It's basically made by mixing spaghetti and chicken with sautéed onion, garlic, bell peppers, and baby bellas in a rich cream-and-cheese sauce, and then baking it. I usually just scrape the mixture into the baking dish and it's perfectly lovely, but when I have a little more time, I use tongs to twirl the spaghetti into nests, as shown. This is excellent with green beans or Romaine Salad with Buttermilk Ranch Dressing and Skillet Croutons (page 125).

PREP: *15 minutes*	**COOK**: *about 1 hour*	**COOL**: *none*

Vegetable oil spray

Kosher salt

1 pound spaghetti

4 tablespoons (½ stick) unsalted butter

½ cup diced (¼-inch) white onion

1 tablespoon minced garlic

1 red bell pepper, finely chopped

1 yellow bell pepper, finely chopped

1 cup trimmed and sliced (½-inch) baby bella mushrooms (from 3 ounces untrimmed)

1 cup heavy cream

½ cup milk

½ cup store-bought chicken broth or Homemade Chicken Broth (page 216)

One 8-ounce block cream cheese, cut into pieces

2 cups grated white Cheddar cheese (about 4 ounces)

2 ounces processed cheese, such as Velveeta, cut into 1-inch pieces

1 teaspoon freshly ground black pepper

2 cups shredded meat from store-bought rotisserie chicken or Poached Chicken Breast (page 85)

2 tablespoons minced fresh parsley, for garnish

1. Preheat the oven to 350°F. Spray a 9 x 13-inch baking pan with vegetable oil.

2. Bring a large pot of generously salted water to a boil. Cook the spaghetti until al dente according to the package directions. Drain thoroughly.

3. Meanwhile, in a deep skillet, melt the butter over medium heat. Add the onion, garlic, and bell peppers and sauté until tender, about 6 minutes. Add the mushrooms and cook for 2 minutes.

4. Stir in the cream, milk, broth, cream cheese, 1 cup of the Cheddar, the Velveeta, 1 teaspoon salt (or to taste), and the pepper. Cook, stirring often, until the cheese is melted and the sauce is creamy. Add the chicken and spaghetti and toss to coat.

5. Transfer to the prepared baking pan. (If desired, use tongs to transfer the spaghetti and swirl each new addition to make little nests, as shown.) Top with the remaining 1 cup Cheddar.

6. Spray one side of a large piece of foil with oil and cover the dish tightly with it. Bake for 20 minutes. Remove the foil and bake until lightly browned, 5 to 10 minutes. (Or, if desired, place under a broiler set to high for 5 to 8 minutes to brown; watch so that it doesn't burn.)

7. Sprinkle with the parsley and serve.

8. Store leftovers in a covered container in the refrigerator for up to 3 days.

Makes 6 to 8 servings

CHICKEN & DUMPLINGS

As soon as the temperature outside drops below 80 degrees my kids start requesting chicken and dumplings for dinner. I'm glad to oblige, although perhaps more so when it's a tiny bit cooler. I gradually developed my own version through years of experimenting with lots of different chicken and dumpling recipes. I kept tweaking various attempts until I landed on this version that I could prepare on a busy weeknight and that yielded generous amounts so we'd have enough leftovers for lunch the next day. When I have extra time, I use homemade chicken broth and fresh biscuit dough.

PREP: *10 minutes*	**COOK:** *40 minutes*	**COOL:** *none*

Two 48-ounce or three 32-ounce cans chicken broth, or 12 cups Homemade Chicken Broth (page 216)

½ cup all-purpose flour, or as needed

Two 16.3-ounce cans refrigerated Pillsbury Grands! Southern Homestyle Original biscuits or ½ recipe dough from Jojo's Biscuits (page 18)

1 cup half-and-half

4 cups shredded meat from 1 store-bought rotisserie chicken or Perfect Roast Chicken (page 203)

1 teaspoon kosher salt, or to taste

1 teaspoon freshly ground black pepper, or to taste

1. In a large (6- to 7-quart) soup pot, bring the broth to a boil over medium-high heat. Reduce the heat to a simmer.

2. Dust a cutting board with some of the flour. Remove the biscuits from the cans and separate them. Place the biscuits on the floured board and cut each one in thirds in one direction and then in thirds at a 90-degree angle to the first cut, to make 9 pieces. As you cut a few biscuits, scrape the pieces and the flour into the simmering broth. Continue to generously flour the board as you cut. (If using fresh biscuit dough, see Note.)

3. Stir in the half-and-half, shredded chicken, and salt and pepper. Cover and simmer gently until heated through and the dumplings are cooked, about 20 minutes. Ladle into bowls and serve hot.

4. Store leftovers in a covered container in the refrigerator for up to 4 days. Reheat gently on the stovetop.

Makes 8 to 10 servings

TIP: *You can stir a bag of frozen mixed vegetables into the broth before adding the biscuits.*

NOTE: *If using fresh biscuit dough, while the broth is coming to a simmer, whisk together the flour and half-and-half to make a slurry. Whisking constantly, pour the slurry into the simmering broth in a slow, steady stream. Continue whisking for 1 minute. Stir in the chicken, salt, and pepper and return to a simmer. Using a 1-ounce scoop or two soup spoons, drop the biscuit dough into the simmering soup. Cover the pan and gently simmer for 25 minutes, until the dumplings are cooked through and dry on top.*

HOMEMADE CHICKEN BROTH

Good-quality boxed chicken broth is a pantry staple for me, but every once in a while, especially on a day when I want to spend a couple of hours in the kitchen preparing lots of different things, I'll make a batch of broth from scratch to store in the freezer. Plus, this method has two-for-one benefits that make it very economical and efficient: It makes a big amount of flavorful broth as well as 3 to 4 cups of shredded cooked chicken.

PREP: *10 minutes*	**COOK**: *2 hours*	**COOL**: *none*

3 pounds whole chicken legs (drumstick plus thigh)
1 white onion, quartered
2 carrots, peeled and halved crosswise
2 celery stalks, halved crosswise

1 teaspoon kosher salt
1 teaspoon black peppercorns
1 bunch parsley and/or thyme
1 bay leaf

1. In a large stockpot, combine the chicken legs, onion, carrots, celery, salt, and peppercorns. Tie the parsley and/or thyme and bay leaf together with kitchen string and add it to the pot. Add 4 quarts cold water.

2. Bring the water to a gentle boil over medium-high heat. Immediately reduce the heat to a gentle simmer. Cook until the chicken is cooked but still has flavor, about 40 minutes. Use tongs to remove the chicken legs to a platter or baking sheet. Let stand just until cool enough to handle with a knife and fork. Remove the meat from the bones. (Set the meat aside to use in another recipe. Store in a covered container in the refrigerator for up to 3 days.)

3. Return the skin and bones to the stockpot and continue to gently simmer for 1 hour. Strain the broth through a mesh sieve and discard the solids.

4. Store the broth in covered containers in the refrigerator for up to 3 days or freeze for up to 2 months.

Makes about 3 quarts

CHICKEN PICCATA
WITH ARTICHOKE HEARTS

Lemon, capers, artichoke hearts, and butter are some of my most favorite ingredients in the world. So it seems like a no-brainer to put all four of them together in a sauce that is spooned over breaded, pan-fried chicken cutlets. My family definitely agrees. And I never mind when one or two of the kids prefer to have their chicken without the sauce because that just leaves more for me.

PREP: *15 minutes*	COOK: *20 minutes*	COOL: *none*

½ cup all-purpose flour

2 large eggs, well beaten

1 cup fine dried bread crumbs

1½ pounds chicken cutlets (see Note)

Kosher salt and freshly ground black pepper

4 tablespoons salted butter, or as needed

2 tablespoons olive oil, or as needed

½ cup white wine or chicken broth

¼ cup fresh lemon juice (from 1 to 2 lemons)

¼ cup capers, drained

1 cup drained marinated quartered artichoke hearts

2 tablespoons caper berries (optional)

3 tablespoons chopped fresh flat-leaf parsley

1 lemon, cut into wedges

1. Spread the flour in a shallow dish. Beat the eggs in a second shallow dish. Spread the bread crumbs in a third.

2. Season the chicken on both sides with 1 teaspoon salt and ½ teaspoon pepper. Lightly and evenly coat the cutlets in the flour, then egg (letting the excess drip away), and then crumbs, pressing lightly to help them adhere. Set aside in a single layer.

3. In a large, heavy skillet, heat 2 tablespoons of the butter and the oil over medium-high heat. Add the cutlets and cook until deep golden brown on both sides and cooked through, turning once with tongs, about 3 minutes on each side. Work in batches if necessary to avoid crowding the skillet, adding more butter and oil as needed.

4. Transfer the cutlets to a serving platter and tent with foil to keep warm.

5. Wipe out the skillet. Add the wine, lemon juice, and capers and simmer until reduced by half, about 4 minutes. Stir in the artichoke hearts and remaining 2 tablespoons butter and stir until the butter melts. Check the seasoning.

6. Spoon the sauce over the chicken, sprinkle with caper berries (if using) and parsley, and garnish with lemon wedges. Serve warm.

7. Store leftovers in a covered container in the refrigerator for up to 3 days.

Makes 4 servings

NOTE: *If the cutlets are more than ¼ inch thick, place them between sheets of plastic wrap and pound with the smooth side of a meat mallet or a heavy rolling pin.*

MRS. GAIL'S CHICKEN & FETTUCCINE ALFREDO

When we were in the thick of busy stretches of filming for our show, it wasn't rare for our dear family friend Gail to offer to make our family a meal. Her crispy breaded chicken cutlets with creamy fettuccine Alfredo is one of our absolute favorites. I always put out lots of extra lemons to squeeze on top of the chicken and serve it with a green salad.

PREP: *30 minutes*	COOK: *45 minutes*	COOL: *none*

CHICKEN

2¼ to 2½ pounds boneless, skinless chicken breasts (about 6 breasts)

Kosher salt and freshly ground black pepper

1 cup all-purpose flour

3 large eggs

1½ cups panko or regular bread crumbs

1½ cups grated Parmesan cheese (about 3 ounces)

½ cup olive oil, or as needed

4 tablespoons (½ stick) salted butter, or as needed

FETTUCCINE ALFREDO

Kosher salt

1 pound fettuccine

8 tablespoons (1 stick) salted butter

3 garlic cloves, minced

2 cups heavy cream

1½ cups grated Parmesan cheese (about 3 ounces)

¼ teaspoon ground white pepper (optional)

FOR SERVING

2 lemons, cut into wedges

1 tablespoon chopped fresh flat-leaf parsley or dried parsley flakes

1. Preheat the oven to 200°F, if desired (see step 5).

2. To make the chicken: Lay a chicken breast on a work surface between two layers of plastic wrap or place it in a sturdy zip-top plastic bag. Gently pound it with a meat tenderizer until it is evenly ¼ to ½ inch thick. Repeat with the remaining breasts. If desired, cut the larger breasts crosswise in half so they're easier to handle. Lightly season them on both sides with salt and pepper.

3. In a large, shallow dish, whisk together the flour, 1 teaspoon salt, and 1 teaspoon pepper. In another large, shallow dish, beat the eggs. In a third large, shallow dish, whisk together the panko and Parmesan.

4. Working with one piece at a time, dredge the chicken in the flour, shaking to remove any excess. Coat the chicken on both sides with the egg. Let the excess run off and then dredge both sides in the panko/Parmesan mixture. Place the chicken on a large baking sheet or platter and continue with the remaining chicken.

continued . . .

continued from page 219

5. Line 1 or 2 large platters or baking sheets with paper towels. In a large skillet, heat ¼ cup of the olive oil and 2 tablespoons of the butter over medium heat until the oil is shimmery and the butter is melted. Place as many pieces of chicken in the pan as can fit without crowding (you may be able to fit only two pieces, which is fine). Fry until golden brown on both sides, about 3 minutes per side. Transfer the chicken to the paper towels. Continue with the remaining chicken, adding more oil and butter as necessary so that there's plenty in the pan for each batch. (If desired, you can place the chicken in the oven while you finish the dish and wipe out the skillet to use for the Alfredo sauce.)

6. Meanwhile, make the fettuccine Alfredo: Bring a large pot of generously salted water to a boil. Cook the fettuccine until al dente according to the package directions. Drain thoroughly.

7. In a large skillet, melt the butter over low heat. Add the garlic and sauté until aromatic and softened, about 2 minutes. Whisk in the cream and cook over low heat, whisking often, until bubbling and slightly thickened, about 6 minutes. Whisk in the Parmesan and white pepper (if using) until melted and well combined. Add the drained pasta to the skillet and use tongs to gently toss until the strands are well coated in the sauce.

8. Serve the fettuccine alongside the chicken. Garnish with lemon wedges and parsley.

9. The chicken's crust will be crispest soon after frying, but leftovers are still tasty and can be stored in a covered container in the refrigerator for up to 3 days.

Makes 6 to 8 servings

BAKED CHICKEN
WITH BACON BOTTOM & WILD RICE

Lining the baking pan with peppered bacon infuses the rice and chicken with its amazing flavor and smokiness, and the kitchen smells so good while this dish bakes. I usually serve this with a good green salad and whatever veggies I have on hand.

PREP: *15 minutes*	COOK: *1 hour and 15 minutes*	COOL: *none*

One 12-ounce package thick-cut peppered bacon

½ white onion, thinly sliced

6 tablespoons salted butter

Three 6.2-ounce boxes Uncle Ben's Long Grain & Wild Rice Fast Cook, cooked according to package directions

One 10.5-ounce can condensed cream of onion or cream of mushroom soup

1 cup sour cream

1 cup store-bought chicken broth or Homemade Chicken Broth (page 216)

1 teaspoon garlic powder

Kosher salt and freshly ground black pepper

2½ pounds chicken tenders

¼ cup chopped chives or parsley, for garnish

1. Preheat the oven to 375°F.

2. Lay the bacon slices side by side to cover the bottom of a 9 x 13 x 3-inch (deep) baking pan or other wide, deep baking dish. Use any remaining slices along the sides of the pan. Place the onion slices on top of the bacon, overlapping them as necessary to cover the bottom. Cut 4 tablespoons of the butter into cubes and evenly sprinkle them on top of the onions.

3. In a large bowl, combine the wild rice blend, soup, sour cream, broth, garlic powder, and salt and pepper to taste. Stir until combined. Spoon the rice over the butter cubes and smooth the mixture out. Nestle the tenders into the rice, pressing them down slightly. Melt the remaining 2 tablespoons butter and brush it on the chicken. Season with a few pinches of salt and pepper.

4. Cover the pan tightly with foil and bake for 55 minutes. Uncover and bake until the chicken is cooked through, about 20 minutes.

5. Sprinkle the chives or parsley on top. Serve right out of the pan.

6. Store leftovers in a covered container in the refrigerator for up to 4 days.

Makes 10 to 12 servings

FRIED CHICKEN

WITH STICKY POPPY SEED JAM

I don't do much deep-frying, but hot fried chicken is so delicious and satisfying to have every once in a while that I think every home cook should have a great recipe for it. Some people may be reluctant to fry at home because it requires a big pot of very hot oil, but it's really pretty easy, and it doesn't require any special equipment. A deep, heavy pot works great. My family prefers white meat so I usually fry halved chicken breasts, but you can do a whole chicken, cut up, or all thighs or all legs—whatever your family likes best. I often pair this fried chicken with green beans and Scalloped Potatoes (page 173).

PREP: *20 minutes, plus overnight soaking (for the chicken)*	**COOK**: *1 hour*	**COOL**: *none*

4 cups buttermilk

2 tablespoons garlic powder

1 tablespoon garlic salt

Freshly ground black pepper

8 pieces bone-in chicken, such as a mixture of drumsticks, thighs, and chicken breasts (halved crosswise)

Vegetable oil, for deep-frying (about 10 cups)

3 large eggs

3 cups all-purpose flour

Kosher salt

Sticky Poppy Seed Jam (page 225), warmed

1. In a large (14-cup) container with an airtight lid, whisk together the buttermilk, garlic powder, garlic salt, and 1 tablespoon pepper. Add the chicken and turn the pieces to coat completely in the buttermilk. Cover the container and refrigerate overnight (see Note).

2. Pour 4 inches oil into a large fryer or deep, heavy pot. Attach a frying or candy thermometer to the side of the pot. Heat the oil over medium-high heat to 350°F.

3. While the oil is heating, whisk the eggs in a shallow dish. In a separate shallow dish, whisk together the flour and 1 teaspoon each salt and pepper. Set a wire rack over a large baking sheet to hold the floured, uncooked chicken and set another wire rack over a baking sheet lined with paper towels to hold the hot fried chicken.

4. Dredge each piece of chicken in the eggs and then in the flour, shaking to remove any excess flour. Set on the rack.

5. When the oil is hot, add a few pieces of chicken to it. Do not crowd the pot. The temperature of the oil will drop as you add the chicken, so adjust the heat as necessary to maintain the oil temperature between 330°F and 350°F (let it go to the lower temperature if the chicken is browning too quickly).

continued . . .

continued from page 223

6. Fry the chicken until the juices run clear when pierced, about 10 minutes. The inside should be cooked thoroughly when sliced open. Use tongs, a spider, or a slotted spoon to transfer the chicken to the wire rack to drain for 5 minutes. Lightly salt the chicken. Return the oil temperature to 350°F. Repeat with the remaining chicken in two or three batches.

7. Transfer to a platter. Serve warm with the poppy seed jam served alongside or drizzled on top.

8. Store the chicken in a covered container in the refrigerator for up to 2 days. Reheat in a 350°F oven for 15 to 20 minutes.

Makes 4 to 8 servings

NOTE: *You don't want to skip the overnight soak. The buttermilk needs time to break down the muscle tissue and make it tender.*

STICKY POPPY SEED JAM

Want to take fried chicken to the next level? Try drizzling the chicken with this sweet and sticky poppy seed jam just before serving. It's also pretty stellar on top of biscuits.

PREP: 5 minutes	**COOK**: under 5 minutes	**COOL**: 15 minutes

1 cup honey (see Tip)
2 tablespoons poppy seeds
1 teaspoon grated lemon zest
1 teaspoon fresh lemon juice

1 teaspoon grated orange zest
1 teaspoon fresh orange juice
½ teaspoon dark brown sugar

1. In a small saucepan, combine the honey, poppy seeds, lemon zest, lemon juice, orange zest, orange juice, and brown sugar and bring to a boil over medium heat, stirring constantly. Remove from the heat and let cool slightly. The jam will thicken as it cools and should appear sticky, like honey.

2. The seeds will separate as the jam sits. Stir well before using. Serve warm.

3. Store in a covered container in the refrigerator for up to 2 days. Warm gently before serving.

Makes 1 cup

TIP: *Spray or rub the measuring cup with vegetable oil before measuring the honey so that it will pour right out without sticking to the sides of the cup.*

FRESH SPINACH & LEEK RISOTTO

I like to make this really lovely dish when we have people over for dinner because it's so pretty. Creamy risotto is filling and satisfying enough to be a full meal, but if you are serving it to someone who doesn't consider anything a full meal without meat, stir in shredded rotisserie chicken. On the other hand, if you want to make it truly vegetarian, use vegetable instead of chicken broth.

PREP: *10 minutes*	**COOK**: *40 to 50 minutes*	**COOL**: *none*

One 32-ounce box store-bought chicken broth or 4 cups Homemade Chicken Broth (page 216)

5 tablespoons salted butter

2 medium leeks (white and light green parts), halved and thinly sliced (about 2 cups)

2 garlic cloves, finely chopped

1 cup short-grain risotto rice, such as Arborio, Carnaroli, or Vialone Nano

½ cup dry white wine or chicken broth

5 ounces baby spinach (about 5 cups)

½ cup grated Parmesan cheese (about 1 ounce), plus more for sprinkling

Finely grated zest and juice of 1 lemon

½ teaspoon ground nutmeg

Kosher salt and freshly ground black pepper

2 tablespoons finely chopped fresh flat-leaf parsley, for garnish

1. In a saucepan, heat the broth and keep it at a bare simmer over low heat.

2. Meanwhile, in a wide, shallow saucepan, melt 4 tablespoons of the butter over medium-low heat. Stir in the leeks and cook, stirring often, until tender, about 5 minutes. Add the garlic and cook, stirring, for 30 seconds.

3. Add the rice and stir until thoroughly coated in the butter. Cook, stirring, until the edges of each grain look translucent and a white dot is visible in the center, about 2 minutes. Stir in the wine and simmer until it cooks away.

4. Ladle ½ cup of the hot broth into the rice. Cook until the rice absorbs the liquid, stirring slowly and constantly.

5. Continue cooking and adding broth in ½-cup increments, stirring until the rice absorbs each addition before adding more. Cook the risotto until the rice is al dente and bathed in thick sauce. Risotto should be creamy but not soupy, as any unabsorbed broth should be thickened by the starch from the rice. The entire process should take 25 to 30 minutes. Be patient and take your time because the longer the rice has to absorb the liquid, the richer and creamier it will be. There might be a little broth left over, or you might need to add a little warm water if you run out of broth.

6. Add the spinach in large handfuls and stir until wilted.

7. Stir in the Parmesan, lemon zest, lemon juice, nutmeg, and remaining 1 tablespoon butter. Season to taste with salt and pepper.

8. Divide among serving bowls. Sprinkle with parsley. Serve immediately, topped with more Parmesan, if you wish.

Makes 4 servings

BOW TIE PASTA
WITH BABY KALE & SUN-DRIED TOMATOES

This creamy pasta dish is a huge crowd-pleaser, packed with all sorts of appetizing ingredients. But I think the thing that makes it really stand out is the toasted walnut and chive topping, which is unexpected and so good. This is perfectly filling and delicious just as is, but you can certainly add 2 cups shredded rotisserie or cooked chicken if desired. I serve it with my Quick Table Salad (page 127).

PREP: *10 minutes*	**COOK**: *30 minutes*	**COOL**: *none*

Kosher salt

1 pound bow tie (farfalle) pasta

2 tablespoons extra virgin olive oil

2 garlic cloves, grated on a rasp grater

2 cups heavy cream

One 8-ounce block cream cheese, cut into pieces

1½ cups bagged shredded Parmesan cheese (about 6 ounces; see Note)

One 12-ounce jar marinated quartered artichoke hearts, drained and halved lengthwise

One 8.5-ounce jar oil-packed sun-dried tomatoes, drained and chopped

5 ounces baby kale or baby spinach (about 5 cups)

Freshly ground black pepper

½ cup chopped walnuts, toasted (see page 79), for garnish

¼ cup minced chives, for garnish

1. Bring a large pot of generously salted water to a boil. Cook the pasta until al dente according to the package directions. Drain the pasta well and return to the pasta pot.

2. Meanwhile, in a large skillet, heat the olive oil over medium heat. Stir in the garlic and sauté for 1 minute. Add the cream and cream cheese and cook, stirring often, until melted. Add the Parmesan and whisk constantly until well blended. Gently stir in the artichokes and sun-dried tomatoes. Add the baby kale and salt and pepper to taste.

3. Pour the cream sauce over the drained pasta and gently toss to coat, taking care not to overstir or break up the pasta.

4. Spoon into bowls and top each with toasted walnuts and chives. Serve hot.

5. Store leftovers in a covered container in the refrigerator for up to 4 days.

Makes 6 servings

NOTE: *For best results and texture here, use shredded rather than grated Parmesan.*

GRILLED SALMON
WITH MEYER LEMONS & CREAMY CUCUMBER SALAD

My family really loves both meat and poultry, but I do serve them fish occasionally as a healthy alternative, and this is one of our favorites. This method is easy and foolproof and it brings out the savory sweetness of salmon. You can use regular lemons here, but if you can find Meyer lemons when they're in season (usually from winter into early spring) it's definitely worth it to pick up a few. Generally smaller and more deeply colored than regular lemons, Meyer lemons' juice is more sweet than acidic, like a cross between a lemon and an orange. Even their zest is distinct—flowery more than citrusy—and they work so perfectly here.

PREP: *15 minutes, plus 1 hour marinating*	COOK: *about 15 minutes*	COOL: *none*

SALMON
Four 6-ounce skin-on wild-caught salmon fillets

½ cup extra virgin olive oil, plus more for grilling

1 tablespoon grated Meyer or regular lemon zest

Juice of 2 Meyer lemons (see head note) or regular lemons, plus 1 or 2 Meyer or regular lemons, sliced into 8 thin rounds

1 tablespoon minced fresh dill

1 tablespoon pink or regular sea salt

CREAMY CUCUMBER SALAD
½ cup mayonnaise, preferably Hellmann's

½ cup sour cream

1 tablespoon fresh Meyer or regular lemon juice, or to taste

1 teaspoon minced fresh dill

1 teaspoon sea salt

½ teaspoon freshly ground black pepper

2 English cucumbers, peeled in stripes, halved, and cut into ¼-inch dice

GARNISH
1 tablespoon minced chives

1. To prepare the salmon: Brush the skin side of the salmon fillets with some olive oil. In a small bowl, combine the ½ cup olive oil, lemon zest, lemon juice, dill, and salt. Pour the mixture into a shallow dish and place the fillets skin side up in the dish. Cover and refrigerate for 1 hour.

2. Meanwhile, prepare the creamy cucumber salad: In a medium bowl, whisk together the mayonnaise, sour cream, lemon juice, dill, salt, and pepper. Fold in the cucumber until completely coated. Taste and adjust the lemon juice or salt. Cover and refrigerate until needed, up to 2 hours.

3. Prepare a medium-hot grill. Lightly oil the grill grate.

4. Place the fillets skin side down on the grill and brush them with the marinade. Cover the grill and cook without flipping until the salmon flakes, 10 to 12 minutes. Brush the lemon slices on both sides with oil and grill until marks appear, 1 to 2 minutes per side.

5. Arrange the fish on individual plates or a serving platter. Place 1 or 2 grilled lemon slices on top of each fillet and dust with chives. Serve with the cucumber salad.

6. Store leftover salmon and cucumber salad in the refrigerator for up to 2 days.

Makes 4 servings

BLACKENED FISH TACOS
WITH RED CABBAGE & MANGO SLAW

Warmed corn tortillas are filled with marinated, spiced, and blackened fish and a tart and slightly sweet, crunchy slaw. The mix of incredible flavors and textures in these tacos makes them impossible to resist, and they are so easy they will make you rethink eating out. I serve these with sliced avocado and warmed seasoned beans.

PREP: *20 minutes, plus 1 to 4 hours resting the slaw and marinating the fish*	COOK: *about 20 minutes*	COOL: *none*

RED CABBAGE & MANGO SLAW

4 cups finely shredded red cabbage (about ¼ medium head)

1½ cups diced (¼-inch) mango (from 1 to 2 mangoes)

1 cup coarsely shredded peeled carrots

Juice of 2 limes

1 tablespoon extra virgin olive oil

1 teaspoon kosher salt

BLACKENED FISH TACOS

1½ pounds skinless halibut, mahi-mahi, turbot, or striped bass fillets

Juice of 1 lime

1 teaspoon hot sauce, preferably Cholula

1 teaspoon smoked paprika

1 teaspoon garlic salt

1 teaspoon freshly ground black pepper

Vegetable oil spray

12 corn tortillas

12 large cilantro sprigs

12 lime wedges

1. To make the red cabbage and mango slaw: In a large bowl, combine the cabbage, mango, carrots, lime juice, olive oil, and salt and toss until well combined. Cover and refrigerate for at least 1 hour and up to 4 hours.

2. To make the blackened fish tacos: Place the fish in a large shallow dish. In a small bowl, combine the lime juice, hot sauce, paprika, garlic salt, and pepper. Coat both sides of each fillet with the sauce. Cover and refrigerate for 30 minutes.

3. Spray a seasoned cast-iron skillet with vegetable oil and heat over high heat until hot (turn on the ventilation fan). Cook the fish until opaque throughout, 3 to 5 minutes per side. (Cook in batches if necessary.) Transfer to a platter, cut into pieces for serving, and set aside.

4. Wipe out the pan and return it to medium-high heat until hot. Heat the tortillas on the pan for 1 to 2 minutes, flipping halfway through, until they are hot and malleable.

5. To build the tacos, divide the fish among the 12 tortillas. Top each with cabbage and mango slaw and then a cilantro sprig. Serve at once with lime wedges.

6. Store the fish and slaw in separate covered containers in the refrigerator for up to 3 days; if storing prepared tacos, store up to 2 days.

Makes 4 to 6 servings

GRILLED RASPBERRY-CHIPOTLE PORK TENDERLOIN

It takes almost no time at all to mix up this marinade, which adds so much flavor. After my first time making this, I now don't do anything else with pork tenderloin. Note that it needs to marinate for 6 to 8 hours for best results. If your family loves it as much as mine does, you may want to grill two tenderloins. There's enough sauce to marinate both if you want to. Use a basting, grilling, or marinating sauce here, not barbecue sauce. If you can't find raspberry-chipotle sauce, look for a different fruit-and-chipotle combination, such as mango or peach.

PREP: 5 minutes, plus 6 to 8 hours marinating	COOK: 15 minutes	COOL: 15 minutes

One 12-ounce bottle raspberry-chipotle sauce, preferably Fischer & Wieser

¼ cup soy sauce

2 tablespoons honey

4 garlic cloves, finely chopped

1 teaspoon garlic powder

1 teaspoon garlic salt

One 1-pound pork tenderloin

Vegetable oil

1. In a medium bowl, whisk together the raspberry-chipotle sauce, soy sauce, honey, garlic, garlic powder, and garlic salt. Add the pork tenderloin to the bowl and turn to coat. Cover and marinate in the refrigerator for 6 to 8 hours.

2. Prepare a medium-hot grill. Oil the grill grate with vegetable oil.

3. Remove the pork from the marinade and place it on the grill. Brush it generously with some of the marinade and discard the remaining marinade. Grill the tenderloin until it reaches 145°F on an instant-read thermometer, about 15 minutes. Use tongs to rotate it a quarter-turn every 3 minutes.

4. Transfer to a cutting board and let rest for 15 minutes. Slice crosswise and serve.

5. Tightly wrap leftover pork in plastic and store in the refrigerator for up to 3 days. Leftover cooked pork can dry out if reheated, but it makes delicious cold sandwiches and a quick taco filling.

Makes 4 servings

COD IN PARCHMENT
WITH LEMON & VEGETABLES

Sealing fish and a few other aromatic ingredients in a parchment paper package is one of the best ways to achieve perfectly cooked white fish with minimal work. And it always makes an impression when the packages are snipped open at the table, revealing the lovely fish and vegetables inside and releasing their amazing aroma. You need only parchment and kitchen string to form the packages and you can serve this with your favorite seasoned rice.

PREP: *20 minutes*	**COOK**: *15 minutes*	**COOL**: *none*

Olive oil, for brushing

Four 6-ounce cod fillets

Kosher salt and freshly ground black pepper

2 lemons, each thinly sliced into 6 rounds

1 small summer squash (about 4 ounces), cut into thin rounds

2 slender carrots (about 4 ounces), peeled and cut into very thin ribbons with a vegetable peeler

1 small fennel bulb, halved, cored, and cut into very thin slices (about 4 ounces)

1 large shallot, finely chopped (about ¼ cup)

4 teaspoons chopped fresh tarragon (optional)

½ teaspoon crushed red pepper flakes

2 garlic cloves, finely chopped

4 tablespoons (½ stick) salted butter

2 tablespoons store-bought chicken broth or Homemade Chicken Broth (page 216)

2 tablespoons dry white wine or more broth

1. Place a large baking sheet on the bottom rack of the oven and remove any other racks (so the packages don't hit them when they puff up). Preheat the oven to 425°F.

2. Arrange four 15-inch squares of parchment paper on a work surface. Brush lightly and evenly with olive oil. Pat the fish dry with a paper towel and place a fillet in the center of each square of paper. Season lightly with salt and pepper. Place 3 lemon slices on top of each fillet. Divide the squash, carrots, and fennel evenly, layering them over the lemons. Season with ¼ teaspoon salt and a pinch of pepper. Sprinkle with the shallot, tarragon (if using), pepper flakes, and garlic. Place 1 tablespoon butter on top of each. Spoon ½ tablespoon broth and ½ tablespoon wine over each.

3. Bring two opposite sides of parchment up over the fennel mixture and fold them together (leave a little headroom). Fold the edges narrowly to seal and tuck them under the package, leaving no openings. Tie closed with kitchen string. Repeat with the rest of the packages.

4. Place the packages directly on the hot baking sheet in the oven and bake for 15 minutes. The paper will puff up and brown. Transfer the packages to serving plates.

5. Serve immediately, snipping open the packages at the table.

6. Store leftovers in a covered container in the refrigerator for up to 1 day.

Makes 4 servings

TIP: *Cooking in parchment is a great way to cook all kinds of delicate, mild fish, such as sole, pollack, haddock, or flounder, in addition to cod.*

MOM'S BULGOGI

My mom grew up in Seoul, South Korea, with a mom who was an amazing cook. I can personally vouch for this because in the 1980s my grandmother and uncle moved in with us in our home in Wichita, Kansas, where I grew up. What I remember most about that time is my grandmother cooking amazing food nonstop. When my grandmother passed away I know my mom regretted never having really learned from her how to cook proper Korean dishes. She ended up adopting a much more American style of cooking and by the time my sisters and I were on the scene, she had long since perfected a few dishes for my steak-and-potato-loving dad. But around that same time she had a lot of Korean friends living nearby, and she learned enough from them that by the time my kids were born, she was often preparing traditional Korean dishes for them, like seaweed soup. It's funny to me that they're growing up eating much more authentic Korean food than I ever did. Mom's bulgogi, though, is more of an American-Korean hybrid, much sweeter than traditional bulgogi, and she serves it on a bed of white rice. Mom has us over once a month and this is what she always makes. It's my kids' very favorite food in the world, so I knew I had to include it in this book. Getting the recipe on paper was a bit of a challenge. My mom had no idea what the measurements were or how to describe what she does, because, as she said, she just does it. (Writing this book made me realize just how alike we are in this way.) But eventually, we figured it out, and I'm so glad we did because now I've captured the blueprint to what will always be a beloved meal for my kids.

We've never had Mom's bulgogi with anything other than her cucumber kimchi salad, which has a clean, fresh flavor that perfectly complements the sweet barbecued beef.

MOM'S BULGOGI
WITH CUCUMBER KIMCHI SALAD

PREP: *20 minutes, plus 4 to 5 hours marinating*	**COOK**: *10 to 20 minutes*	**COOL**: *none*

BULGOGI

1½ cups packed light brown sugar

1 cup soy sauce

5 tablespoons sparkling dessert wine, such as Banfi Rosa Regale, or sparkling grape juice

3 tablespoons sesame oil

2 green onions (light and dark green parts), chopped, plus ¼ cup sliced for serving

2 garlic cloves, chopped

1 teaspoon freshly ground black pepper

4 to 5 pounds beef tenderloin, rib-eye, top sirloin, or sirloin steak, thinly sliced (see Note)

CUCUMBER KIMCHI SALAD

2 English cucumbers, peeled if desired, cut into ½-inch dice

2 green onions (light and dark green parts), thinly sliced on the diagonal

2 garlic cloves, minced

1 to 2 teaspoons gochugaru (Korean red pepper flakes; see Tip)

2 teaspoons sugar

1 teaspoon rice vinegar

1 teaspoon sesame oil

½ to 1 teaspoon kosher salt, to taste

FOR SERVING

Steamed white rice

1 to 2 tablespoons thinly sliced green onion (light and dark green parts) as needed, for garnish

3 tablespoons sesame seeds, toasted (see page 79), for garnish

1. Marinate the bulgogi: In a large bowl, whisk together the brown sugar, soy sauce, wine, sesame oil, green onions, garlic, and pepper until well combined. Add the beef and coat it completely in marinade. Cover and refrigerate for 4 to 5 hours.

2. To make the cucumber kimchi salad: In a medium bowl, combine the cucumbers, green onions, garlic, gochugaru, sugar, vinegar, sesame oil, and salt to taste and stir gently. Cover and refrigerate until ready to serve.

3. Prepare a hot grill. If the pieces of beef are so small that they may fall through the grates, use a grilling skillet or place a sheet of foil on the grill.

4. Grill the beef on both sides until medium-well, 3 to 5 minutes, flipping halfway through cooking. Don't crowd the skillet or foil, so do this in batches if necessary. As you finish each batch, transfer it to a serving platter and continue with the remaining beef.

5. Serve the bulgogi on top of steamed rice. Garnish with green onion and toasted sesame seeds and spoon the cucumber kimchi salad alongside.

6. Store the leftover bulgogi and cucumber kimchi salad in separate covered containers in the refrigerator for up to 3 days.

Makes 6 to 8 servings

NOTE: *My mom usually has the butcher slice the beef for this dish when she buys it. If you live near a Korean market, they often sell packages of sliced rib-eye or top sirloin; sometimes they're even marked specifically for bulgogi. If you buy big pieces to cut yourself, freeze the meat for about 30 minutes before cutting so that it's easier to slice thinly and cut against the grain.*

TIP: *Gochugaru, or Korean red pepper, is commonly used in kimchi. It adds precisely the right amount of heat and unique flavor to the cucumber salad. Authentic Korean brands are readily available at Asian grocery stores or online, and the McCormick spice company packages it as well.*

JO'S FATAYAR

When I was a kid we went to my grandparents' house after church almost every Sunday and my granddad would make meat pies and Lebanese salad. (The meat pies are called fatayar, which my family has always pronounced "fatay.") My grandparents had nine children and a ton of grandchildren, so as you can imagine Sunday lunch at Grandma and Grandpa's was a big event. After my granddad passed away, Dad would reminisce about watching his father make these meat pies, grating all the potatoes by hand, mixing the dough from scratch, and lovingly filling each pie.

When I had kids of my own I set out to re-create Grandpa's meat pies in a way that my kids would love them, too. I remembered that it felt like it took hours for my granddad's pies to cook, because he used raw meat and then by the time it was cooked, the biscuit was very crisp. So I streamlined the recipe, including cooking the meat before filling the pies so that I can take them out of the oven when the biscuit is perfectly baked without worrying about the meat. I skip the potato grating and dough mixing by using frozen shredded hash browns and our favorite store-bought biscuit dough. And I always add lots of cheese, no surprise there.

Now, every year on his birthday, Dad requests my fatayar and Lebanese salad, with his favorite, Rice Krispies treats, for dessert. He truly considers this the perfect meal and that makes me really happy. Though I've made plenty of revisions to Grandpa's recipe, I think he would be so pleased that this tradition lives on in such an important way for our family.

Gradually our kids decided that they, too, wanted to adopt the tradition, requesting this exact meal for their own birthdays. It has become infinitely more than mere food to all of us. When I make fatayar and Lebanese salad I'm not only feeding my family; I'm also honoring them. That somehow continues to feel deeply personal and profound to me, and for that I am thankful.

JO'S FATAYAR
WITH LEBANESE SALAD

PREP: *30 minutes*	COOK: *40 minutes*	COOL: *none*

LEBANESE SALAD

4 large vine-ripened tomatoes, cut into ¼-inch dice

4 English cucumbers, cut into ¼-inch dice

½ cup minced white onion (optional)

Juice of 1 lemon

¼ cup extra virgin olive oil

1 teaspoon kosher salt

½ teaspoon freshly ground black pepper

FATAYAR

1 tablespoon extra virgin olive oil

¼ cup minced white onion

2 pounds ground beef (80% lean)

2 cups thawed frozen shredded hash browns

2 cups bagged grated Cheddar cheese (about 8 ounces)

1 teaspoon kosher salt

1 teaspoon garlic salt

1 teaspoon freshly ground black pepper, plus more as needed

Three 16.3-ounce cans refrigerated Pillsbury Grands! Southern Homestyle Original biscuits

All-purpose flour, for the work surface

4 tablespoons (½ stick) salted butter, melted

GARNISH

2 teaspoons dried parsley flakes

1. To make the Lebanese salad: In a medium bowl, combine the tomatoes, cucumbers, onion (if using), lemon juice, oil, salt, and pepper. Toss gently until well combined. Cover and refrigerate for up to 8 hours.

2. Position racks in the top third and middle of the oven and preheat the oven to 350°F. Line two baking sheets with parchment paper.

3. To make the fatayar: In a large sauté pan, heat the oil over medium-high heat. Add the onion and cook, stirring often, until softened, about 3 minutes. Add the beef and cook, stirring often to break up the meat, until no longer pink, about 6 minutes. Pour off any standing liquid. Stir in the hash browns, Cheddar, salt, garlic salt, and the pepper. Stir until well combined. Taste and adjust the seasoning. Set aside.

4. Open the cans of biscuits and separate the dough into individual biscuits (24 total). Dust a work surface with some flour. Roll out each biscuit to a roughly 5½-inch round.

5. Working with one round at a time, place about ¼ cup meat filling in the middle, leaving a roughly ½-inch border all around. Bring the sides of the dough up in three parts and pinch together the three seams from the base up to the top center so that the package forms a triangle. It is fine if the meat peeks through at the top.

6. Continue to fill and pinch all the biscuit rounds, arranging the pies on the prepared baking sheets as you form them and placing them close together so that they all fit.

7. Brush the tops with the melted butter and sprinkle a little kosher salt on the top.

8. Bake until golden, about 30 minutes, switching racks and rotating the pans halfway through baking so that the pies bake evenly.

9. Garnish the salad with parsley flakes and serve the fatayar hot with the salad.

10. Store leftover fatayar and salad in separate covered containers in the refrigerator for up to 3 days.

Makes 24 fatayar; 8 to 10 servings

SHEPHERD'S PIE

There's an excellent reason this dish has been a favorite comfort food for generations. Seasoned ground beef, bright green beans, and the mashed potatoes that I dream about are layered and baked together so that every bite is a mix of great flavors and textures. Plus, it's a complete meal in a single baking dish, and it can be put together up to a day in advance, all of which makes it ideal for the busyness of life. I like to serve this with warm rolls and butter.

PREP: *15 minutes*	**COOK**: *under 1 hour*	**COOL**: *none*

Vegetable oil spray

Kosher salt

2½ pounds russet potatoes (about 6 medium), peeled and cut into 1½-inch chunks

½ cup milk

½ cup heavy cream

2 tablespoons salted butter

1 teaspoon ground nutmeg

1 pound green beans, ends snapped, cut into 2-inch pieces

1 tablespoon vegetable oil

1 small white onion, cut into ¼-inch dice

1 garlic clove, minced

2 carrots, peeled and cut into ½-inch dice

1 bay leaf

2 pounds ground beef (80% lean)

2½ tablespoons all-purpose flour

3 tablespoons tomato paste

2 tablespoons hot water

1½ teaspoons Worcestershire sauce

Freshly ground black pepper

2 tablespoons minced parsley or chives, for garnish

1. Preheat the oven to 350°F. Spray a 9 x 13-inch baking pan with vegetable oil.

2. Bring a large pot of generously salted water to a boil. Add the potatoes and cook until tender when pierced with a knife, 15 to 20 minutes. Drain and return the potatoes to the pot.

3. Mash the potatoes using a potato masher, adding the milk, heavy cream, butter, nutmeg, and ½ teaspoon each of salt and pepper, mashing as you go, until they are creamy, smooth, and well blended. Keep warm aside.

4. Meanwhile, in a pot with a steamer insert or in a covered sauté pan fitted with an expandable steamer basket, bring 2 inches of water and 1 tablespoon kosher salt to a boil. Add the green beans to the steamer insert or basket, cover, and steam until crisp-tender, about 8 minutes. Rinse with cold water to stop the cooking, drain well, and set aside.

5. In a large skillet, heat the oil over medium-high heat. Stir in the onion, garlic, carrots, and bay leaf and cook until the vegetables begin to soften, 6 to 7 minutes. Add the beef and cook, stirring often to break up the meat, until no longer pink, about 10 minutes. Pour off any standing liquid.

6. Push the ingredients to one side of the skillet and add the flour, tomato paste, hot water, Worcestershire sauce, 1 teaspoon salt, and ¾ teaspoon pepper. Stir until blended, then combine with the beef/carrot mixture in the pan. Cook until the mixture is thickened, 3 to 5 minutes. Remove from the heat. Remove and discard the bay leaf.

7. Spread the meat mixture in the prepared baking pan and layer the green beans on top.

8. Scrape or spoon the potato mixture over the green beans and smooth the top. (If desired, you may cover the pan and refrigerate for up to 1 day before baking. Let stand at room temperature for 1 hour before baking.)

9. Bake until heated through and the potatoes are lightly browned on top, 30 to 40 minutes.

10. Sprinkle with parsley or chives. Serve hot, straight from the baking dish.

11. Store leftovers in a covered container in the refrigerator for up to 3 days.

Makes 6 to 8 servings

BEEF TENDERLOIN

WITH PICKLED JALAPEÑO SOUR CREAM

Beef tenderloin is a splurge, for sure, so I choose it for important occasions and I prepare it carefully. I begin by marinating it for at least 8 hours. Then, to roast it, I put it into an extremely hot oven for a few minutes and then turn the oven off and let it stay for several minutes without opening the oven door. This unusual roasting method seals in great flavor and cooks the meat perfectly. It's very important to follow the directions as written and not open the oven door once you've put the roast in, to avoid allowing too much heat to escape. We always have pickled jalapeños around; you can use my recipe (on page 255) to make your own or use store-bought. I love using both brine and pickles here. The jalapeño brine in the marinade helps to tenderize the beef, and the jalapeños themselves add a nice kick to the sour cream served with the roasted tenderloin. I buy a fully trimmed and tied tenderloin from the store so I can put it directly in the marinade. If your tenderloin is untrimmed, you can ask the butcher to do it for you, or you'll need to do a little trimming before you begin. Trim away any excess fat using a sharp knife. And be sure to remove the thin, shiny silverskin with a knife; if you don't, what should be a soft-as-butter loin will be tough and elastic. Tie the loin at even intervals and you're ready to go.

BEEF TENDERLOIN
WITH PICKLED JALAPEÑO SOUR CREAM

PREP: *20 minutes, plus at least 9 hours marinating and standing*	COOK: *about 35 minutes*	COOL: *15 minutes*

BEEF TENDERLOIN

½ cup soy sauce

½ cup Worcestershire sauce

½ cup brine from Pickled Jalapeños (page 255)

2 tablespoons Montreal steak seasoning

One 3- to 3½-pound center-cut beef tenderloin, trimmed and tied

2 tablespoons salted butter, at room temperature

PICKLED JALAPEÑO SOUR CREAM

2 cups sour cream

3 tablespoons drained and finely chopped pickled jalapeños (see Tip), or to taste (page 255)

Kosher salt and freshly ground black pepper

1. Marinate the beef tenderloin: Pour the soy sauce, Worcestershire sauce, jalapeño brine, and steak seasoning in a large zip-top plastic bag. Add the tenderloin, squeeze out the air, and close tightly. Refrigerate for at least 8 hours, preferably overnight. Turn the bag from time to time to help the roast marinate evenly.

2. Remove the tenderloin from the bag and discard the marinade. Blot the roast dry with paper towels and let stand at room temperature for 1 hour.

3. Meanwhile, make the pickled jalapeño sour cream: In a small bowl, stir together the sour cream, jalapeños, and salt and pepper to taste. Cover and refrigerate for at least 1 hour before serving.

4. Position a rack in the middle of the oven and preheat the oven to 500°F. Line a baking sheet with foil.

5. Place the tenderloin on the lined baking sheet and spread the butter over the top.

6. Roast for 9 to 11 minutes (3 minutes per pound). Turn off the oven. Leave the roast in the oven for 20 minutes for medium-rare (125°F on an instant-read thermometer) or 25 minutes for medium (130°F on an instant-read thermometer). Do not open the oven door.

7. Transfer to a cutting board and let rest for 15 minutes before slicing.

8. Tightly wrap leftover beef in plastic and store in the refrigerator for up to 3 days. Leftover cooked beef makes delicious cold sandwiches. Store leftover jalapeño cream in a covered container in the refrigerator for up to 3 days.

Makes 8 servings

TIP: *You can replace the jalapeños in the sour cream mixture with an equal amount of prepared horseradish if you prefer a more traditional pairing.*

PICKLED JALAPEÑOS

Of all our kids, Duke is by far the most interested in the garden. He understands that there's a lot of work involved and he considers the rewards to be worth it. I never have to ask him to go into the garden to get things for me, because usually he's already been out there picking what's ready before I get home from work. Some days, as I'm walking in the door, he's running to me with his shirt pulled out in front of him holding whatever bounty he's just picked. And whenever the jalapeños are ripe, he gets so excited to help me pickle a big batch.

One of my absolute favorite parts of parenting is figuring out how to connect with each of my kids individually. Thanks to their distinct personalities, different things interest each of them. For Duke and me, it's the garden and, more specifically, it's pickling jalapeños together. The funny thing is, he doesn't even like spicy food, and he's never actually eaten the pickled jalapeños. Chip, on the other hand, puts them on anything and everything he can. What matters to Duke is simply the time we spend together in the kitchen tending to the chiles he's picked, which makes me love this activity as much as he does.

We typically pickle about twenty jalapeños at a time, usually once a month during the season. That gives us around eight little jars. I keep two jars for the family (mostly for Chip) and I give the rest away over the course of the month, because I think everyone could use a little pickled jalapeño in their life.

PICKLED JALAPEÑOS

PREP: *15 minutes*	COOK: *20 minutes*	COOL: *5 hours, plus at least 3 days pickling*

3 cups distilled white vinegar

6 tablespoons sugar

3 tablespoons kosher salt

1 garlic clove, smashed

20 large jalapeños (about 1¼ pounds), sliced into ⅛-inch-thick rings (see Tip)

1. Have ready six to eight ½-pint (8-ounce) jars with tight-fitting lids. Clean them in the dishwasher or in hot soapy water.

2. In a large saucepan, combine 3 cups water, the vinegar, sugar, salt, and garlic. Bring the mixture to a boil over high heat. Stir in the jalapeño slices and cook until they turn from bright green to a slightly duller green, about 7 minutes.

3. Use a slotted spoon to transfer the jalapeños to the jars, dividing them equally among the jars (leave the garlic behind). Spoon the pickling liquid into each jar, filling each to ½ inch below the rim.

4. Cover the jars tightly. Let cool completely, then store in the refrigerator for up to 2 weeks. You can use pickled jalapeños right away, but they get tastier and less spicy the longer they sit. We usually wait for about 3 days before using them.

Makes six to eight 8-ounce jars

TIP: *The compound in chiles that makes them hot is called capsaicin, and it can be painful if you get it on your hands. To protect them, wear disposable rubber gloves when cutting chiles. I recommend chopping chiles on a dishwasher-safe cutting board that goes directly into the dishwasher when you're done and washing your knife thoroughly before using it to chop other ingredients.*

GAINES FAMILY CHILI

This is one of the recipes my sister-in-law included in the Gaines family cookbook she gave me when Chip and I were first married. It's super easy and great for company. The Fritos and shredded cheese on top are a revelation, so you won't want to skip those. If you can't find Ranch Style brand Southwestern-style beans, use your favorite canned chili beans instead.

PREP: *5 minutes*	COOK: *about 45 minutes*	COOL: *none*

1 tablespoon vegetable oil
1 large white onion, finely chopped
2 pounds ground beef (80% lean)
Kosher salt and freshly ground black pepper
Two 10-ounce cans mild diced tomatoes and green chiles, such as Ro*tel, undrained

Two 26-ounce cans Southwestern-style beans, preferably Ranch Style brand, undrained
One 10.25-ounce bag Fritos
2 cups grated sharp Cheddar cheese (about 8 ounces)
Jalapeño Cornbread (page 262)

1. In a large soup pot or Dutch oven, heat the oil over medium heat until hot. Add the onion and sauté until translucent and tender, about 8 minutes.

2. Add the beef and a couple of pinches each of salt and pepper and cook, stirring often to break up the meat, until it loses its pink color, 6 to 7 minutes.

3. Stir in the tomatoes and beans with their juice. Bring to a simmer, reduce the heat, and simmer, stirring occasionally, for 30 minutes. Taste and adjust the seasoning.

4. Ladle the chili into bowls. Serve topped with Fritos and grated Cheddar and accompanied by cornbread.

5. Store leftovers in a covered container in the refrigerator for up to 4 days.

Makes 6 to 8 servings

BEEF ENCHILADAS

These beef enchiladas don't require much work and they're always a big hit. Serve with
Mexican Rice (page 195) or your favorite seasoned rice and Apple Cider Salad (page 119).

PREP: *15 minutes*	**COOK**: *45 minutes*	**COOL**: *10 minutes*

Vegetable oil

1 medium onion, finely chopped

1 pound ground beef (80% lean)

1 tablespoon chili powder

1 teaspoon ground cumin

Kosher salt

¼ teaspoon freshly ground black pepper

1 cup canned or frozen diced Hatch or other green chiles

8 corn tortillas

1½ cups red enchilada sauce

2 cups grated Mexican blend or sharp Cheddar cheese (about 8 ounces)

¼ cup thinly sliced green onions (light and dark green parts), for serving

Sour cream, for serving

1. Preheat the oven to 350°F.

2. In a large skillet, heat 1 teaspoon oil over medium heat. Stir in the onion and cook until it begins to soften, about 5 minutes. Add the beef and cook over medium-high heat, stirring often to break up the meat, until no longer pink, about 5 minutes. Pour off any standing liquid. Stir in the chili powder, cumin, ½ teaspoon salt, and the pepper. Cook, stirring, for 1 minute. Remove from the heat and stir in the green chiles.

3. In a medium skillet, heat 2 tablespoons oil over medium-high heat until it is hot but not smoking. Line a plate with paper towels. Fry a tortilla for about 10 seconds on each side, using tongs to flip it. Transfer to the paper towels and very lightly season with salt. Continue with the remaining tortillas, stacking them between paper towels as you pull each one out of the skillet. Add a little more oil to the pan if necessary, waiting until it is hot before continuing.

4. Spread ¼ cup of the enchilada sauce in a 9 x 13-inch baking dish. Pour about ½ cup of the enchilada sauce onto a plate.

5. Working with one tortilla at a time, place it in the sauce on the plate to coat the bottom. Spread about ⅓ cup of the meat mixture down the center, sprinkle with a little cheese, and roll up the tortilla. Place it seam side down in the baking dish. Repeat to form a total of 8 rolls, nestling them against one another in the dish. Pour the remaining sauce over the rolls, then sprinkle the remaining cheese over the top.

6. Bake until browned on top and gently bubbling around the edges, about 30 minutes. Let stand for 10 minutes.

7. Serve warm, passing the green onions and sour cream at the table.

8. Store leftovers in a covered container in the refrigerator for up to 3 days.

Makes 4 servings

MEAT LOAF

There's really no way to make a loaf of meat look pretty, but this tastes so good that it's easy to overlook its homely appearance. Meat-and-potato people like Chip and my dad absolutely love this recipe, and a good meat loaf is a great dish to have in the dinner rotation. I add crushed crackers for the nice texture they contribute and the kids like it when I brush the top with ketchup before baking. Mixing in a bit of finely chopped and sautéed onion adds a pleasing, extra layer of flavor; use the smaller amount as called for in the recipe or leave it out entirely if it's not something your family cares for. I serve this with Becki's Mac & Cheese (page 169), a salad or green beans tossed with melted butter, and warm rolls.

PREP: 15 minutes	**COOK**: 1 hour 10 minutes	**COOL**: 10 minutes

2 tablespoons salted butter
¼ to ½ cup finely chopped onion, to taste
1½ pounds ground beef (85% lean)
1 sleeve (4 ounces) saltines, crushed
1½ cups grated Cheddar cheese (about 6 ounces)

2 large eggs, beaten
½ cup tomato sauce
1 teaspoon Worcestershire sauce
1½ teaspoons kosher salt
¼ teaspoon freshly ground black pepper
2 tablespoons ketchup

1. Preheat the oven to 350°F.

2. In a large skillet, melt the butter over medium-low heat. Add the onion and sauté until translucent, about 5 minutes. Remove from the heat and let cool.

3. In a large bowl, combine the beef, cooled onion, saltine crumbs, Cheddar, eggs, tomato sauce, Worcestershire sauce, salt, and pepper. Use your hands to gently mix the ingredients together until well blended. Try to keep a light touch and not overwork the mixture.

4. On a 9 x 13-inch or other large baking pan, form the mixture into a roughly 6 x 9-inch loaf.

5. Drizzle the ketchup down the center of the loaf and brush it over the top to cover.

6. Bake until firm (170°F on an instant-read thermometer), about 1 hour. Let stand 10 minutes before slicing. Serve warm.

7. Store leftovers in a covered container in the refrigerator for up to 4 days.

Makes 4 to 6 servings

BEEF STEW

WITH JALAPEÑO CORNBREAD

As soon as the weather turns cool my family starts longing for this hearty stew. It's one of my favorite Sunday traditions during the fall. I like to prep it in the morning and let it simmer all day. Then in the evening I quickly bake the cornbread and soon we have a warm and welcoming meal that tastes and feels just like autumn.

PREP: *15 minutes*	COOK: *under 2 hours*	COOL: *none*

1 pound beef stew meat, cut into 1½-inch chunks

Kosher salt and freshly ground black pepper

4 tablespoons (½ stick) salted butter

1 white onion, cut into ¼-inch dice

4 carrots, peeled and cut into ¼-inch dice

3 celery stalks, cut into ¼-inch dice

¼ cup all-purpose flour

1 tablespoon garlic powder

1 tablespoon garlic salt

One 32-ounce box beef broth

One 14.5-ounce can fire-roasted diced tomatoes

One 14.4-ounce can gold and white corn, such as Del Monte, undrained

1 large russet potato, scrubbed and cut into ¾-inch cubes

1 cup frozen peas

Jalapeño Cornbread (page 262), for serving

1. Lightly season the beef with a pinch each of salt and pepper. In a large soup pot, heat the butter over medium heat until the foam subsides. Add the beef and sauté it until browned on all sides, about 10 minutes.

2. Add the onion, carrots, and celery and sauté until the vegetables are tender but not fully cooked, about 10 minutes. Stir in the flour, garlic powder, garlic salt, and 1 teaspoon each of kosher salt and pepper. Cook for 1 or 2 minutes, stirring occasionally, until well combined.

3. Add the broth, tomatoes, corn and its liquid, and potato. Add up to 1 cup water if necessary to ensure that the ingredients are covered. Bring to a boil over medium-high heat. Reduce the heat to a simmer, cover, and cook until the meat and potatoes are tender, about 1 hour 15 minutes.

4. Add the frozen peas and simmer, uncovered, until the peas are cooked but still bright, 5 to 10 minutes. Ladle the stew into bowls. Serve immediately with the cornbread on the side.

5. Store leftovers in a covered container for up to 5 days or in the freezer for up to 1 month.

Makes 8 to 10 servings

JALAPEÑO CORNBREAD

I love how quickly I can mix up the batter for this and then pop it in the oven to serve with dishes like Beef Stew (page 261) and Gaines Family Chili (page 256) that just don't feel complete without warm cornbread and softened butter.

PREP: *5 minutes*	**COOK:** *50 minutes*	**COOL:** *none*

4 tablespoons (½ stick) unsalted butter, melted and cooled, plus softened butter for the skillet and for serving

1 cup all-purpose flour, sifted

1 cup fine stone-ground yellow cornmeal

1 teaspoon kosher salt

½ teaspoon garlic powder

1 cup heavy cream

2 large eggs

1 cup drained canned white corn

¼ cup chopped drained pickled jalapeños (optional; page 255)

¼ cup chopped drained roasted pimientos (optional)

1. Position a rack in the top third of the oven and preheat the oven to 375°F. Butter a 10-inch cast-iron skillet.

2. In a large bowl, whisk together the flour, cornmeal, salt, and garlic powder.

3. In a medium bowl, whisk together the melted butter, cream, and eggs.

4. Add the liquid ingredients to the flour mixture along with the corn and the jalapeños (if using) and pimientos (if using). Stir until moistened but not overmixed; the batter will be thick.

5. Scrape the batter into the prepared skillet and smooth the top. Bake until the top is lightly browned, the edges are browned, and a tester inserted in the center comes out clean, about 50 minutes.

6. Slice the warm cornbread into 6 wedges and serve at once with pats of butter.

7. Cornbread is best the day it is made. Wrap leftovers tightly in foil and store at room temperature for up to 3 days. Reheat by slicing and toasting or broiling.

Makes 6 servings

SUNDAY SUPPER BEEF TIPS

Chip and the kids are always happy when they see me tossing the ingredients for this dish into the slow cooker on a Sunday morning. The sherry adds some acidity, but my kids prefer it without, so I usually skip it. The beef is tender and great either way. I serve this with saffron-seasoned rice and my Quick Table Salad (page 127).

PREP: *10 minutes*	**COOK:** *8 hours in the slow cooker*	**COOL:** *none*

One 10.5-ounce can condensed cream of mushroom soup

One 1-ounce package onion soup mix

⅓ cup dry sherry (optional)

2 pounds lean stew beef, cut into 2-inch cubes

½ teaspoon freshly ground black pepper

8 ounces cremini or baby bella mushrooms, trimmed and cut into ½-inch-thick slices (about 2½ cups), or one 4-ounce can sliced mushrooms, drained

Cooked seasoned saffron rice or your favorite rice mix, for serving

1. In a slow cooker, combine the cream of mushroom soup and onion soup mix. If using sherry, add it along with ⅓ cup water; if not using sherry, add ⅔ cup water. Whisk together until well combined.

2. Season the beef with the pepper. Add it to the slow cooker along with the mushrooms and stir to coat.

3. Cover and cook on low for 8 hours, until the beef is tender.

4. Serve hot with saffron rice or other seasoned rice.

5. Store leftover beef and rice in covered containers in the refrigerator for up to 3 days.

Makes 4 to 6 servings

- CHAPTER 7 -

Desserts

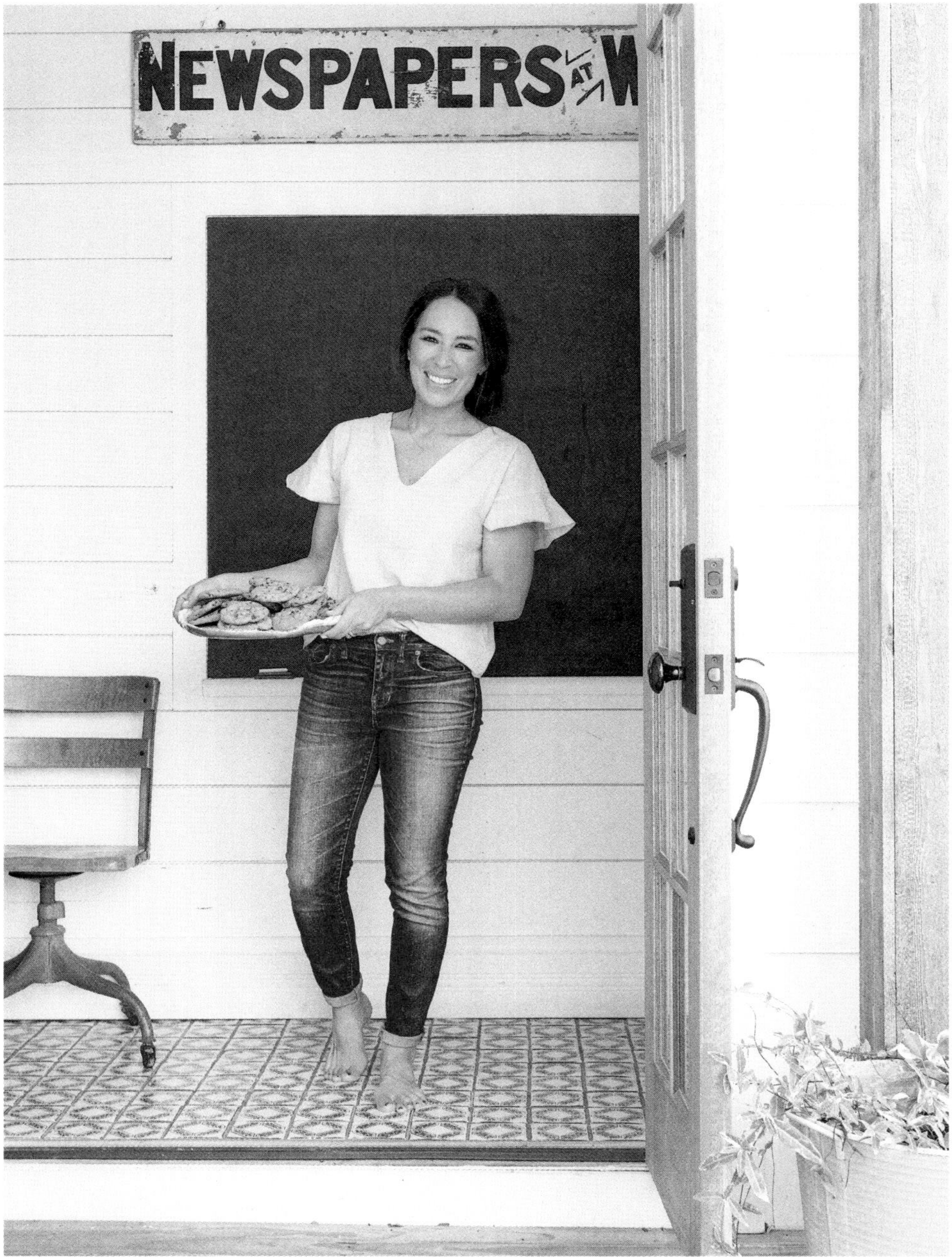
NEWSPAPERS AT

DESSERTS

I like to say that serving dessert after dinner makes a well-balanced meal, and my kids never seem to argue with me on that point. I always crave something sweet after a savory dinner, and the kids seem to take after their mama! But for me there's more to it than just how much I enjoy eating sweets (although that really can't be overstated). Of all the types of cooking I do, preparing desserts and baking make me feel the most nostalgic in the best possible way. Cutting butter into flour to make a pie crust or mixing up a batch of cookie dough makes me feel really knit into my family—my kids, parents, grandparents, and all the generations that came before them. This is probably part of why I've always liked to keep that cake stand on my kitchen counter full of something freshly made and delicious. To me, baking is a tangible expression of the profound love and gratitude I feel for my family and friends.

This means that when I go into the kitchen and bust out all the pots and pans for dinner, I almost certainly plan to prepare a sweet afterward as well. But I don't believe that desserts need to be fancy or complicated. Most of my favorites are easy to prepare, and my pantry quite literally always includes the makings for a handful of them. I typically have on hand no fewer than three bags of chocolate chips (it never occurs to me to buy just one bag at a time), nuts, graham crackers for crusts, cocoa, lemons, and plenty of butter, eggs, flour, and sugar so I can always whip something up even if I haven't planned ahead. And with make-ahead options like Key lime or lemon and lavender icebox cookies, filling the house with amazing aromas is as simple as slicing and baking some cookie dough.

The recipes that follow are all favorites of my family. Each of the kids has his or her preference, the ones that they shout out first when I ask them what I should make for dessert. Invariably, at least one person wants lemon pie, brownie pie, or chocolate chip cookies. If it were up to me the chocolate-cola cake would always be in the house, and Chip would be happiest with strawberry shortcake on biscuits, since that's the closest thing to breakfast in this chapter. I really hope that you and your family will also find some favorites to love. And remember, if anyone you know is worried about the extra calories that come with dessert, tell them there is always the option of skipping breakfast, lunch, or dinner!

LEMON PIE

I remember early on in my marriage a friend of mine shared this simple recipe with me, and I couldn't believe how delicious it was for the little amount of work it required. There's something about the blend of a graham cracker crust, lemon filling, and fresh whipped cream that makes for a perfect dessert. Plus, it's really beautiful!

PREP: *20 minutes*	**COOK**: *under 20 minutes*	**COOL**: *1½ hours*

LEMON PIE

Vegetable oil spray

1½ cups crushed graham crackers (from about 27 squares)

⅓ cup sugar

6 tablespoons salted butter, melted

3 cups sweetened condensed milk

3 egg yolks

⅔ cup fresh lemon juice (from 3 to 4 lemons)

Pinch of sea salt

WHIPPED CREAM TOPPING

1 cup heavy cream

2 tablespoons sugar

1 teaspoon pure vanilla extract

GARNISH

Lemon slices

Grated lemon zest

Mint sprigs

1. To make the lemon pie: Preheat the oven to 350°F. Lightly spray a 9-inch pie plate with vegetable oil.

2. In a large bowl, combine the crushed graham crackers and ⅓ cup of the sugar and stir to blend. Stir in the melted butter until well blended. Press the cracker mixture onto the bottom and up the sides of the prepared pie plate. Bake until firm, about 8 minutes.

3. Meanwhile, in a stand mixer fitted with the paddle attachment (or in a large bowl with a handheld electric mixer), beat the condensed milk, egg yolks, lemon juice, and salt on medium speed for 4 minutes.

4. Pour the mixture into the baked pie crust. Return to the oven and bake until the center is set when the pan is gently nudged, about 10 minutes.

5. Cool the pie on a rack for 30 minutes. Place in the refrigerator until set, at least 1 hour and up to 3 days.

6. Just before serving, make the whipped cream topping: In a medium bowl, with a handheld electric mixer, beat the cream, sugar, and vanilla on high speed until fluffy and the cream holds a soft peak when you pull the beater out of the bowl.

7. Spread the cream on the cooled pie. Garnish with fresh lemon slices, a sprinkle of lemon zest, and mint sprigs.

Makes 8 servings

PEACH & ALMOND TART
WITH WHIPPED MASCARPONE

When I have the time to make an extra-special dessert for a summertime dinner party, I love to make this tart. I poach peaches in sugar syrup, then slice and nestle them in a rich almond filling inside a tart shell. After baking, I top the cooled tart with whipped sweetened mascarpone and cream. It's truly incredible. Mascarpone is the Italian version of cream cheese that is familiar to many people as an integral ingredient in tiramisu. It is available at Italian markets and many supermarkets.

PREP: *45 minutes*	**COOK**: *under 1 hour*	**COOL**: *1 hour*

CRUST

Dough from Pie Crust (page 28) or store-bought pie dough

Softened butter, for the tart pan

POACHED PEACHES

2 cups sugar

Grated zest and juice of 1 lemon

1 pound peaches, halved and pitted

ALMOND FILLING

6 tablespoons salted butter, at room temperature

½ cup sugar

2 large eggs

¾ cup almond flour or finely ground almonds

½ teaspoon almond extract

TOPPING

¼ cup peach preserves

½ cup mascarpone cheese, at room temperature (see Tip)

½ cup heavy cream, at room temperature (see Tip)

2 tablespoons powdered sugar

⅛ teaspoon almond extract

2 tablespoons sliced almonds, lightly toasted (see page 79) and cooled

1. To prepare the crust: Roll the dough to a 14-inch round. Butter the bottom and sides of a 10-inch tart pan with a removable bottom. Gently lay the rolled crust over the tart pan, taking care not to stretch it. Lift the edges of the dough with one hand, and with your other hand, press the dough into the bottom of the pan and gently up the sides. Roll a rolling pin over the top of the tart pan to cut off the excess dough around the outside edge. Place in the refrigerator while you prepare the filling.

2. To poach the peaches: In a medium saucepan, combine 2 cups water, the sugar, lemon zest, and lemon juice. Bring to a simmer over medium heat. Add the peach halves skin side up and simmer until the skin begins to pucker and the fruit is just tender when pierced with a knife, about 5 minutes. Transfer the peaches with a slotted spoon to a plate to cool slightly. Slip off and discard the skins. Reserve 2 tablespoons of the poaching liquid and discard the rest or strain and refrigerate for another use.

3. Preheat the oven to 375°F.

4. To make the almond filling: In a medium bowl, with an electric mixer, beat the butter and sugar on high speed until creamy. Add the eggs one at a time, beating well after each addition. Beat in the almond flour and extract. Spread into the bottom of the chilled tart shell.

5. Cut the peaches into thin slices and arrange the slices in concentric circles over the filling.

6. Drizzle the reserved poaching liquid over the fruit.

7. Bake until the filling is set and golden brown and the crust is golden, 40 to 45 minutes. Cool to room temperature on a wire rack.

8. To make the topping: In a small saucepan, melt the preserves over low heat, about 5 minutes. (Alternatively, combine the preserves with 1 tablespoon water in a glass measuring cup and heat in the microwave for 30 seconds.) Strain through a fine-mesh sieve and discard the solids. Brush the warm strained preserves on top of the tart.

9. In a medium bowl, with an electric mixer, beat the mascarpone, cream, powdered sugar, and almond extract on high speed to soft peaks.

10. Spoon the whipped mascarpone over the tart. Sprinkle the cream with the toasted almonds. Serve at room temperature or lightly chilled.

11. Cover leftover tart and store at room temperature for up to 1 day.

Makes 8 servings

TIP: *The mascarpone and cream should both be at room temperature before beating them together for the topping. If one or both are too cold, they might curdle.*

DULCE DE LECHE APPLE PIE

Dulce de leche is sweetened milk that has been gently cooked until it is thickened, caramel-y, and, in summary, heavenly. It's so good baked inside this old-fashioned favorite, with even more drizzled on top. A common issue people have when they bake apple pie is the amount of liquid the apples give off while the pie bakes. It used to drive me crazy, especially because even if I made the pie the same way every time, when I'd cut into it, sometimes there wasn't much liquid and other times it was like the apples were swimming in the deep end of a pool. I finally realized that the best way around this was to cook the apples on the stovetop for a bit before transferring them to the pie shell. I do this with a slotted spoon to ensure that most of the liquid stays behind. Now I don't hold my breath when I cut into my apple pie wondering what it will look like under the top crust. Instead, what I always find is fragrant, perfectly cooked apples.

PREP: 25 minutes	**COOK**: 1 hour 30 minutes	**COOL**: 1 hour

Dough for 2 Pie Crusts (page 28) or a store-bought 9-inch double-crust deep-dish pie crust

4 tablespoons (½ stick) salted butter

½ cup packed light brown sugar

¼ cup granulated sugar

1 teaspoon ground cinnamon

¼ teaspoon ground allspice

¼ teaspoon ground nutmeg

5 pounds Honeycrisp, Golden Delicious, and/or Braeburn apples, peeled and thinly sliced (about 12 cups)

¼ cup all-purpose flour

¼ cup dulce de leche, plus warmed dulce de leche for serving

1 tablespoon milk

1 tablespoon coarse raw (turbinado) sugar

2 pints vanilla ice cream, for serving

1. Lightly dust the counter with flour and roll one dough out to a round 3½ inches larger than a 9-inch deep-dish pie plate. Transfer the dough to the pie plate and carefully ease it into the edges of the plate. Trim the dough to an even ½ inch all around and leave the overhang. For the top pastry round, roll the second dough out to a round that is big enough to allow a 1/2-inch overhang all around. Transfer it to a baking sheet. Refrigerate it and the lined pie plate until needed.

2. In a large saucepan, heat the butter over medium-high heat. When foaming, stir in the brown sugar, granulated sugar, cinnamon, allspice, and nutmeg. Gently stir in the apples. Cover and cook until the apples begin to soften and the liquid comes to a boil.

3. Stir in the flour. Continue cooking until the apples are almost tender, 5 to 10 more minutes. Do not let the apples turn soggy or begin to break apart. Remove from the heat and cool to room temperature.

4. Preheat the oven to 425°F.

continued . . .

continued from page 273

5. Use a slotted spoon to transfer the filling to the pie shell, mounding the apples in the center. Drizzle ¼ cup of the cooking liquid over the apples. Heat ¼ cup dulce de leche in the microwave for about 30 seconds until pourable, then drizzle it over the apples.

6. Cover the pie with the top pastry round, turn under the edges, and crimp closed. Brush the top crust lightly and evenly with the milk and then sprinkle with the raw sugar. Cut six 2-inch slits in the top crust to release steam.

7. Bake for 25 minutes. Reduce the oven temperature to 325°F and continue baking until the crust is deep golden brown and juices bubble through the steam vents, about 45 more minutes. Shield the edge of the crust with foil if it browns too quickly.

8. Cool to room temperature on a wire rack to set the filling before cutting. (Reheat the pie at 350°F for about 20 minutes if you would like to serve the pie warm.)

9. Serve at room temperature or warm topped with ice cream and warm dulce de leche.

10. Cover leftover pie and store at room temperature for up to 2 days.

Makes one 9-inch pie; 8 servings

SPICED PECAN PIE

It's funny how a small tweak to a classic recipe can make it seem completely new and exciting. I'm not saying traditional pecan pie needs improving, but adding a bit of ground ancho chile creates a sweet-and-heat pairing that sends this pie into another stratosphere. I serve it with whipped cream and a dusting of ground cinnamon.

PREP: *10 minutes*	**COOK**: *1 hour*	**COOL**: *1 hour*

1 cup packed light brown sugar

1 cup light corn syrup

3 tablespoons salted butter, melted

3 large eggs

2 teaspoons ground cinnamon, plus more for serving

2 teaspoons ancho chile powder

2 cups coarsely chopped pecans (see Note)

1 unbaked deep-dish Pie Crust (page 28) or a store-bought 9-inch deep-dish pie crust

Homemade Whipped Cream (page 285) or good-quality store-bought whipped cream

1. Preheat the oven to 350°F.

2. In a large bowl, whisk together the brown sugar, corn syrup, and butter. Whisk in the eggs. Whisk in the cinnamon and ancho powder. Stir in the pecans.

3. Pour into the pie crust.

4. Bake until the filling puffs around the edges and is nearly set in the center, about 1 hour. A knife inserted 2 inches from the center should come out clean. Cool to room temperature on a wire rack.

5. Serve at room temperature or lightly chilled with a dollop of whipped cream dusted with cinnamon.

6. Cover leftover pie with plastic wrap and store in the refrigerator for up to 2 days.

Makes 8 servings

NOTE: *I typically use coarsely chopped pecans here because it's much easier to cut neat slices of the pie. You can use an equal amount of halved pecans if you prefer, and even arrange them in concentric circles if you have the time and desire.*

BROWNIE PIE

*Two of my kids' most favorite desserts in the world are brownies and pie. The first time
I made this they thought I was some kind of miracle worker. This really is the best of both
worlds: rich brownies with chocolate chips and nuts baked into a flaky pie crust.*

PREP: *25 minutes*	**COOK**: *1 hour*	**COOL**: *1 hour*

8 tablespoons (1 stick) salted butter

2 ounces unsweetened chocolate, coarsely
chopped

1 cup sugar

3 large eggs

½ cup all-purpose flour

1 teaspoon pure vanilla extract

¼ teaspoon kosher salt

1 cup (6 ounces) semisweet chocolate chips

½ cup coarsely chopped pecans

1 unbaked Pie Crust (page 28) or a store-bought
9-inch deep-dish pie crust

Powdered sugar, for garnish

1. Preheat the oven to 350°F.

2. Heat the butter and unsweetened chocolate in a small saucepan over low heat, stirring until
melted and smooth.

3. Remove the pan from the heat and whisk in the sugar until smooth. Pour into a medium bowl
and set aside to cool for 10 minutes.

4. Whisk in the eggs one at a time. Whisk in the flour, vanilla, and salt.

5. Fold in the chocolate morsels and pecans. Pour into the pie crust.

6. Bake until just set and a crust forms on top, about 1 hour. Cool to room temperature on a wire
rack.

7. Just before serving, dust with powdered sugar.

8. To store, wrap tightly and keep at room temperature for up to 2 days.

Makes 8 servings

CHERRY-ALMOND CRISP

One of my absolute favorite combinations, both in taste and smell, is cherry and almond. This crisp comes together in minutes and tastes so good, especially when it's warm and topped with vanilla ice cream. I really like that I can make it year-round, using fresh sweet cherries in season and defrosted frozen ones the rest of the year.

PREP: *15 minutes*	**COOK**: *20 minutes*	**COOL**: *20 minutes*

TOPPING

1 cup rolled oats
¾ cup packed light brown sugar
½ teaspoon ground cinnamon
½ teaspoon ground ginger
6 tablespoons salted butter, cut into bits, at room temperature, plus more for the ramekins
½ cup slivered almonds

FILLING

2 pounds fresh sweet cherries, pitted, or thawed frozen cherries, blotted dry (about 5 cups)
Finely grated zest of 1 lemon
2 tablespoons fresh lemon juice
1 teaspoon almond extract
½ cup granulated sugar
¼ cup cornstarch

FOR SERVING

1½ pints vanilla ice cream

1. To make the topping: In a medium bowl, stir together the oats, brown sugar, cinnamon, and ginger. Use a pastry cutter to work the butter into the oat mixture until pebbly. Gently stir in the almonds. Freeze until needed.

2. Preheat the oven to 375°F. Butter six 10-ounce ramekins and set them on a rimmed baking sheet.

3. To make the filling: In a large bowl, stir together the cherries, lemon zest, lemon juice, and almond extract.

4. In a small bowl, stir together the granulated sugar and cornstarch. Sprinkle the mixture over the cherries and toss to coat. Divide among the prepared ramekins.

5. Divide the topping among the ramekins, covering the cherries.

6. Bake on the baking sheet until the topping is deep golden brown and juices bubble around the edges, about 20 minutes.

7. Cool at least 20 minutes, then serve warm or at room temperature with ice cream.

8. Cover leftovers and store in the refrigerator for up to 3 days.

Makes 6 servings

BROILED HONEY-THYME PEACHES
WITH ICE CREAM & AGED BALSAMIC

This lovely sweet-and-savory dessert is perfect for dinner guests when peaches are in season. I love the slightly sweet finish of good-quality balsamic vinegar, but balsamic that has been aged over a decade takes it to the next level. I don't use this rich, syrupy vinegar in vinaigrettes. Rather, I like to save it for drizzling on fresh fruit and cheese.

PREP: *10 minutes*	COOK: *under 10 minutes*	COOL: *none*

4 tablespoons (½ stick) salted butter, melted, plus softened butter for the baking dish

4 peaches, peeled, halved, and pitted

¼ cup honey

¼ teaspoon freshly ground black pepper

1 teaspoon fresh thyme leaves

1 pint vanilla ice cream

2 tablespoons aged balsamic vinegar

1. Position a rack in the middle of the oven and turn the broiler to high. Butter a 9 x 13-inch baking dish.

2. Arrange the peach halves cut side down in the dish. Broil until browned in spots, about 3 minutes, watching carefully to keep them from burning. Flip the peaches over. Drizzle with the melted butter and the honey and sprinkle with the pepper. Broil until browned and bubbling, 4 to 5 more minutes.

3. Remove from the oven and sprinkle with the thyme.

4. Scoop ice cream into dessert bowls. Divide the peaches and the pan juices over the ice cream. Drizzle with balsamic and serve at once.

Makes 4 servings

STRAWBERRY SHORTCAKE

Chip's favorite way to eat biscuits is with jam and gravy, but mine is in strawberry shortcake. This classic doesn't need much of an introduction, but if you've never had sweetened ripe strawberries spooned over soft, buttery biscuits with homemade whipped cream, you're in for a real treat.

PREP: *15 minutes,* *plus 1 hour standing*	COOK: *none*	COOL: *none*

2 pounds strawberries, hulled and quartered
½ cup sugar
6 Jojo's Biscuits (page 18)

Homemade Whipped Cream (recipe follows)
    or good-quality store-bought whipped cream
6 small mint sprigs, for garnish

1. In a medium bowl, toss the strawberries with the sugar. Set aside at room temperature for up to 1 hour.

2. Split the biscuits in half. Arrange the bottom halves on each of 6 plates.

3. Layer whipped cream and strawberries on each biscuit. Place the remaining biscuit halves on top. Garnish with mint. Serve.

Makes 6 servings

HOMEMADE WHIPPED CREAM

I probably make fresh whipped cream at least once a week, no matter the season, since it's just as delicious topped on ice cream as it is on a warm fruit crisp. Even on nights when I don't have time to prepare a full dessert, I'll still whip cream to put on top of a store-bought pie or cake. It only takes a few minutes (four, to be exact, with my electric mixer) and it makes everything it touches better.

PREP: *under 5 minutes*	COOK: *none*	COOL: *none*

1 pint heavy cream
¼ cup sugar

1 teaspoon pure vanilla extract
Pinch of sea salt

1. In a large bowl, combine the cream, sugar, vanilla, and salt. Beat with an electric mixer on high speed until fluffy and the cream holds a soft peak when you pull the beater out of the bowl.

2. Use at once or store in a covered container in the refrigerator for up to 30 minutes.

Makes about 4 cups

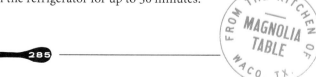

AUNT OPAL'S BANANA PUDDING

Chip's great-aunt Opal didn't have children of her own, but she cooked a lot for Chip's dad and uncle when they were kids. She was especially known for her excellent pies and this spectacular banana pudding. When Chip and I were first married, it was a staple of his mom's and we usually enjoyed it on Christmas Eve. I've loved it ever since. When I make this family favorite, I typically use my homemade whipped cream in place of dessert topping, but either is great. I usually compose the whole thing in a clear glass trifle dish so the pretty layers are visible. You can serve it in individual cups if you prefer.

PREP: *20 minutes, plus at least 2 hours chilling*	**COOK**: *none*	**COOL**: *none*

One 8-ounce block cream cheese, at room temperature

One 14-ounce can sweetened condensed milk

1 cup whole milk

One 3.4-ounce package instant vanilla pudding

6 cups Homemade Whipped Cream (page 285) or one 16-ounce tub Cool Whip, thawed

One 11-ounce box vanilla wafers

3 bananas, sliced, or as needed

1. In an electric stand mixer fitted with the whisk attachment (or in a large bowl with a handheld electric mixer), beat the cream cheese until smooth. Add the condensed milk, regular milk, and pudding mix. Beat on high speed for about 2 minutes, until very well blended. Add half of the whipped cream and beat just until combined.

2. To assemble the pudding, use a 3-quart trifle bowl or other straight-sided glass bowl. (As shown in the photo, this can also be assembled as individual servings; see Note.) Cover the bottom of the bowl with vanilla wafers, arranging them in a single layer without overlapping. Spoon about one-third of the pudding on top to a depth of about 1½ inches. Cover the pudding with a layer of wafers. Arrange a layer of banana slices on top of the wafers.

3. Spoon half of the remaining pudding on top of the banana slices to a depth of about 1½ inches above the first layer. Again, cover the pudding with a layer of wafers and then arrange a layer of banana slices on top.

4. Spoon the remaining pudding over the bananas and smooth the top. Cover the pudding with a layer of wafers.

5. Spoon the remaining whipped cream on top and smooth the surface or use the back of a spoon to form pretty swirls on the surface before serving.

6. Cover the bowl with plastic wrap and chill in the refrigerator for at least 2 hours and up to 1 day.

Makes 6 to 8 servings

NOTE: *Layer the ingredients, following the same order, into six to eight 8-ounce clear glasses.*

MOCHA TRIFLE CUPS

Chip doesn't generally like chocolate desserts, but he loves these layered mousse cups. Whenever I serve these to him, he's always a little hesitant, and then happily surprised all over again. "Oh yeah!" he'll say every time. "I really like these!" I don't know if it's the bit of coffee in the mousse or its velvety texture, but he's a fan—even if he doesn't always know it. As for me, I never struggle to remember that I love chocolate. And this dessert gets additional bonus points because it's beautiful and it can be prepared ahead of time. When I make these, I put all the trifle cups on a pretty serving tray in the fridge so that when I'm ready to serve, I can remove them all at once and top each one with whipped cream and mint.

PREP: *30 minutes, plus at least 1 hour chilling*	COOK: *none*	COOL: *none*

One 9-ounce package chocolate wafer cookies or 24 Oreos

One 12-ounce package semisweet chocolate chips

½ cup sugar

2 tablespoons instant coffee powder

Pinch of kosher salt

7 large eggs, separated (see Note)

1 teaspoon pure vanilla extract

Homemade Whipped Cream (page 285) or good-quality store-bought whipped cream

8 to 10 small mint sprigs, for garnish

1. Place the cookies in a food processor and pulse until crushed. Set aside.

2. In a large saucepan, combine the chocolate chips, sugar, coffee powder, salt, and 5 tablespoons water and cook over medium heat until the chocolate is melted and the mixture is smooth, stirring often. Remove the pan from the heat.

3. Meanwhile, in a large bowl, whisk together the egg yolks and vanilla.

4. Whisking constantly, add about ¼ cup of the hot chocolate mixture to the yolks to temper them. Beat with an electric mixer to blend. Pour the remaining chocolate into the bowl and beat until well blended.

5. In a separate, very clean large bowl, with an electric mixer beat the egg whites until stiff. Fold them into the chocolate mixture, taking care not to overmix.

6. Spread half the cookie crumbs in the bottoms of eight 8- to 10-ounce individual serving glasses.

7. Using half the mousse, evenly divide among the glasses, spooning it on top of the crumbs. Sprinkle the remaining crumbs on top. Divide the remaining mousse among the glasses. Chill in the refrigerator for at least 1 hour and up to 1 day.

8. Just before serving, top each glass with whipped cream and garnish with a mint sprig.

Makes 8 servings

NOTE: *The eggs in this mousse are not cooked. If you're concerned about the potential for salmonella, use eggs that have been pasteurized in the shell to minimize the risk.*

BUTTERMILK BLUEBERRY PUFF

I think this tastes like the very best blueberry muffins, blueberry pie, and blueberry pancakes all combined into one baking dish. It's as fantastic for breakfast as it is for dessert when we have a crowd. It doesn't matter what time of day it is, the serving dish is always empty at the end of the meal.

PREP: *15 minutes*	COOK: *35 minutes*	COOL: *none*

12 tablespoons (1½ sticks) unsalted butter, at room temperature, plus 1 tablespoon for the baking dish

12 cups cubed croissants (6 to 8 large)

3 cups blueberries or blackberries

1 cup granulated sugar

6 large eggs, at room temperature

2 cups heavy cream

1 cup buttermilk

2 tablespoons pure vanilla extract

1 teaspoon kosher salt

1 tablespoon coarse raw (turbinado) sugar

1. Preheat the oven to 375°F. Grease a 9 x 13 x 3-inch (deep) baking dish with the 1 tablespoon butter.

2. Spread the croissant cubes evenly in the dish. Top with the berries.

3. In a stand mixer fitted with the paddle attachment (or in a large bowl with a handheld electric mixer), beat the 12 tablespoons butter with the granulated sugar on medium speed until creamy. Beat in the eggs, one at a time, beating well after each addition. Beat in the cream, buttermilk, vanilla, and salt (the mixture may appear curdled).

4. Pour over the croissants and berries in the baking dish. Sprinkle with the coarse sugar.

5. Bake until a knife inserted near the center comes out clean, about 35 minutes. Serve warm.

6. The puff is best eaten warm, soon after baking, but leftovers can be covered and stored in the refrigerator for up to 2 days.

Makes 12 servings

CHOCOLATE-ORANGE BREAD PUDDING

Bittersweet chocolate and orange have a natural affinity. Each makes the other tastier than either could be alone. I especially love how they complement each other in this rich bread pudding, which is simultaneously comforting and elegant.

PREP: *20 minutes, plus 30 minutes standing*	COOK: *55 minutes*	COOL: *15 minutes*

Butter, for the baking dish

One 1-pound loaf French bread, torn into bite-size pieces (about 10 cups)

4 large eggs

4 large egg yolks

3 cups heavy cream

½ cup Grand Marnier (orange liqueur) or orange syrup

½ cup plus 2 tablespoons sugar

Finely grated zest and juice of 1 orange

Seeds from ½ split and scraped vanilla bean or 1 teaspoon pure vanilla extract

½ teaspoon kosher salt

8 ounces bittersweet (60% cacao) chocolate, coarsely chopped

Homemade Whipped Cream (page 285) or good-quality store-bought whipped cream

2 cups chopped Candied Pecans (page 294)

1. Preheat the oven to 350°F. Generously butter a 9 x 13-inch baking dish.

2. Evenly spread the bread in the prepared pan. Set aside.

3. In a large bowl, whisk together the whole eggs and egg yolks until well blended. Whisk in the cream, Grand Marnier, ½ cup of the sugar, orange zest, orange juice, vanilla seeds or extract, and salt.

4. Pour the liquid evenly over the bread, making sure that all of the bread is covered in some liquid. Let stand for 30 minutes, stirring occasionally and pressing the bread into the liquid. Fold in the chocolate pieces, making sure that the chocolate is well distributed throughout and not all at the bottom of the dish. Sprinkle with the remaining 2 tablespoons sugar.

5. Bake until a knife inserted in the center comes out clean, about 55 minutes. Let stand on a wire rack for 15 minutes, then serve warm, topped with whipped cream and candied pecans.

6. Store leftovers in a covered container in the refrigerator for up to 3 days.

Makes 12 to 16 servings

CANDIED PECANS

These sweet, buttery, crunchy pecans are great sprinkled on top of warm bread pudding or ice cream. They're similar to the Buttered Walnuts or Pecans (page 123) that I use in my salads, and can be used the same way.

PREP: *under 5 minutes*	**COOK**: *10 minutes*	**COOL**: *30 minutes*

4 tablespoons (½ stick) salted butter
¼ cup lightly packed light brown sugar
2 cups pecan halves

1. In a cast-iron skillet, melt the butter over medium heat. Add in the brown sugar and stir until well combined.

2. Add the pecans and stir to completely coat them in the butter. Cook, stirring frequently, until toasted, about 8 minutes.

3. Scrape onto a sheet of wax paper and let cool to room temperature. Break apart as necessary before using.

4. Store in an airtight container at room temperature for up to 4 days.

Makes 2 cups

CHOCOLATE-COLA CAKE
WITH CHOCOLATE-COLA BUTTERCREAM

Chocolate cake with ice cream is a pretty common craving of mine. When I choose to succumb, this is the cake I usually make and it always hits the spot. My kids know I have a sweet tooth, of course, but I think even they're surprised when they come home from school and find an almost full frosted sheet cake waiting for them. That's only possible because of how quickly it comes together . . . and the powerful pull of chocolate.

PREP: *30 minutes*	COOK: *40 to 45 minutes*	COOL: *1 hour*

CAKE

Nonstick baking spray or vegetable shortening, for the pan

2 cups all-purpose flour

1 cup granulated sugar

1 cup packed dark brown sugar

½ teaspoon kosher salt

½ pound (2 sticks) salted butter

¼ cup natural unsweetened cocoa powder

1 cup cola (not diet)

1 teaspoon baking soda

½ cup buttermilk, at room temperature

2 large eggs, at room temperature, lightly beaten

1 teaspoon pure vanilla extract

FROSTING

12 tablespoons (1½ sticks) salted butter, at room temperature

½ cup natural unsweetened cocoa powder, sifted

¼ cup cola (not diet)

2 cups powdered sugar, sifted

1. To make the cake: Preheat the oven to 350°F. Spray a 9 x 13-inch baking pan with baking spray or grease with vegetable shortening.

2. In a large bowl, whisk together the flour, granulated sugar, brown sugar, and salt.

3. In a small saucepan, bring the butter, cocoa, and cola to a boil over medium-high heat, stirring until smooth. Pour into the flour mixture and whisk until smooth.

4. In a small bowl, dissolve the baking soda in the buttermilk. Pour into the flour mixture and whisk until smooth. Whisk in the eggs and vanilla.

5. Pour the batter into the prepared pan and bake until a tester inserted in the center comes out clean, 40 to 45 minutes. Cool in the pan on a wire rack.

6. To make the frosting: In a stand mixer fitted with the paddle attachment (or in a large bowl with a handheld electric mixer), beat the butter on medium speed until smooth. Add the cocoa and cola and beat on low speed until smooth. Scrape the bowl. Beat in 1 cup of the powdered sugar on medium speed. Scrape the bowl. Beat in the remaining 1 cup powdered sugar on medium speed. Scrape the bowl. Spread over the cooled cake before slicing and serving.

7. If any cake is left over, cover the pan tightly and store at room temperature for up to 2 days.

Makes 12 servings

BEVIE'S CHOCOLATE ROLL
WITH HOT FUDGE SAUCE

This cake has been a dessert centerpiece at the Gaines family Thanksgiving table for twenty-five years. Chip's mom (the kids call her Bevie) jokes that we fight over it, and she's not totally kidding. It's all I can do not to skip the turkey and go straight for the chocolate roll before anyone notices. I've never managed to make it as well as Bevie, but I knew I had to share this recipe with you because it's that delicious. I mean it, this is a tricky recipe, but it's worth it! And worst-case scenario, if you fail, you can easily turn the roll into a fabulous trifle. Crumble the cake and layer it with whipped cream and hot fudge sauce in a large bowl. So without further ado, here it is: Bevie's famous chocolate roll. I hope you enjoy it as much as we always do—whether it's Thanksgiving or not.

PREP: 40 minutes, plus at least 4 hours chilling	**COOK**: under 25 minutes	**COOL**: none

4 large eggs, separated
1 cup granulated sugar
2 tablespoons cold water
1 tablespoon pure vanilla extract
⅓ cup all-purpose flour
⅓ cup natural unsweetened cocoa powder
1 teaspoon baking powder

¼ teaspoon sea salt
¼ cup powdered sugar, plus more for serving
One 8-ounce container whipped dessert topping, such as Cool Whip, thawed
Hot Fudge Sauce (page 298)
Homemade Whipped Cream (page 285) or good-quality store-bought whipped cream

1. Preheat the oven to 325°F. Line the bottom and sides of a 10 x 15-inch jelly-roll pan with parchment paper.

2. In the very clean large bowl of a stand mixer fitted with the whisk attachment, beat the egg whites until stiff. Beating constantly, gradually add ½ cup of the granulated sugar and continue beating until the whites hold a stiff peak when the beaters are lifted straight out of the bowl.

3. In a separate large bowl, with a whisk beat the egg yolks with the remaining ½ cup sugar, the cold water, and the vanilla. Fold in the egg whites and gently stir to combine. Do not overmix.

4. Sift the flour, cocoa powder, baking powder, and salt on top of the egg mixture and gently fold until blended. Scrape the batter into the prepared pan and spread it to the edges.

5. Bake until the cake is puffy on top and the center is firm when gently patted with a finger, 18 to 22 minutes. Let cool in the pan for 2 minutes.

6. Dust a clean kitchen towel with the ¼ cup powdered sugar. Unmold the chocolate roll onto the towel with the parchment paper still attached. Starting at one short end, carefully roll the cake

continued . . .

continued from page 297

up at the same time that you pull the parchment paper off; you can use a small knife and run it between the paper and the cake to help separate the two if necessary. (See photos a–d.)

7. When the cake is rolled all the way up and the parchment paper is removed, immediately unroll the cake, again using a small knife to help separate the cake if it sticks. Spread the dessert topping all over the surface of the cake and roll it up again. Use a sharp or serrated knife to cut off the ends so the roll has clean edges. (See photos e–i.)

8. Cover and refrigerate for at least 4 hours and up to 1 day.

9. Just before serving, sprinkle powdered sugar on top. Cut into roughly 1-inch-wide slices. To serve, place a slice on a plate, drizzle with the hot fudge sauce, and top with a dollop of whipped cream.

Makes 8 servings

TIP: *The cake can be made one day in advance, which makes it especially nice for holidays.*

HOT FUDGE SAUCE

This chocolate sauce is great over the cake as well as on top of ice cream and fruit, so if you have some left over, just refrigerate it until another use presents itself.

PREP: *5 minutes*	COOK: *5 minutes*	COOL: *none*

¾ cup sugar
½ cup evaporated milk, plus more as needed
2 tablespoons salted butter

2 tablespoons light corn syrup
Pinch of sea salt
½ cup milk chocolate chips

1. In a saucepan, combine the sugar, evaporated milk, butter, corn syrup, and salt and cook over medium heat, stirring constantly, until the sugar is melted. Add the chocolate chips and stir until melted. Remove from the heat and use at once or set aside until needed. (The sauce can be stored in the refrigerator for up to 1 week.)

2. Gently reheat in a saucepan over low heat if necessary. Serve warm.

Makes about 2 cups

LEMON BUNDT CAKE

I've always appreciated the ease of making Bundt cake. You mix some simple ingredients together and throw them in a pan, and the delicious result far exceeds what you could reasonably expect for the amount of effort required. This moist, tangy lemon cake with a sweet-tart lemon glaze is no exception. In fact, it's one of my very favorites.

PREP: 25 minutes	**COOK**: 50 to 55 minutes	**COOL**: 1 hour

CAKE

Nonstick baking spray or softened butter, for the pan

3 cups all-purpose flour (plus more for the pan if not using baking spray)

Grated zest of 2 lemons

½ teaspoon baking soda

½ teaspoon sea salt

½ pound (2 sticks) unsalted butter, at room temperature

2 cups granulated sugar

4 large eggs

1 cup buttermilk

LEMON GLAZE

1 cup powdered sugar

1 to 2 tablespoons fresh lemon juice, or as needed

1. To make the cake: Preheat the oven to 350°F. Spray a 12-cup Bundt pan with nonstick baking spray or butter and flour the pan.

2. In a medium bowl, whisk together the flour, lemon zest, baking soda, and salt. Set aside.

3. In a stand mixer fitted with the paddle attachment (or in a large bowl with a handheld electric mixer), beat the 2 sticks butter and granulated sugar on medium-high speed until light and fluffy, 3 to 5 minutes. Scrape down the sides of the bowl. Add the eggs one at a time, beating well after each addition.

4. Turn the mixer to low speed and alternately add the flour and buttermilk, beginning and ending with the flour. Mix just until incorporated.

5. Spoon the batter into the prepared pan. Shake the pan gently and knock it once or twice firmly on the counter to settle any bubbles.

6. Bake until a tester inserted midway between the edge and the center tube comes out clean, 50 to 55 minutes.

7. Cool in the pan on a rack for 30 minutes, then unmold onto the rack to cool completely.

8. Meanwhile, make the lemon glaze: Sift the powdered sugar into a medium bowl. Whisk in enough lemon juice to make a soft glaze that drips in a wide ribbon off the whisk.

9. Place the cake on a serving plate. Drizzle the glaze over it.

10. To store leftover cake, wrap it tightly in plastic or foil and keep at room temperature for up to 1 day.

Makes 12 to 14 servings

LEMON ANGEL FOOD CAKE
WITH FRESH BLUEBERRY COMPOTE

The airy texture and delicate flavor of angel food cake make me feel as if I'm eating a cloud. The only thing that could enhance such a magical thing is lemon, so I add plenty of grated zest and a small amount of lemon extract. I serve the cake topped with fresh blueberry compote and homemade whipped cream. For best results, use store-bought pasteurized egg whites, which whip up beautifully and are very stable.

PREP: *25 minutes*	**COOK**: *45 to 50 minutes*	**COOL**: *1 hour*

CAKE

1 cup cake flour

2 cups sugar

1½ cups egg whites (from 10 to 12 large eggs)

⅛ teaspoon sea salt

1½ teaspoons cream of tartar

1 tablespoon lightly packed grated lemon zest (from 1 large lemon)

1 teaspoon pure vanilla extract

1 teaspoon lemon extract

COMPOTE

1½ cups good-quality blueberry preserves, such as Bonne Maman

Juice of 1 lemon

2 pints fresh blueberries

FOR SERVING

Homemade Whipped Cream (page 285) or good-quality store-bought whipped cream

1. To make the cake: Position a rack in the center of the oven and preheat the oven to 350°F.

2. Sift the flour and ½ cup of the sugar into a medium bowl. Repeat the sifting twice more.

3. In the very clean bowl of a stand mixer fitted with the whisk attachment, beat the egg whites, salt, and cream of tartar on low speed until combined and opaque. Increase the speed to high and gradually add the remaining 1½ cups sugar. Beat to stiff, glossy peaks.

4. Add the lemon zest, vanilla, and lemon extract and beat on medium speed to combine, about 1 minute.

5. Add the flour mixture in fourths, sprinkling it over the beaten whites and folding it in gently with a rubber spatula.

6. Scrape the batter into a 10-inch angel food pan (aluminum tube pan with a removable bottom, see Tip). Smooth the top and bake until the cake is deep golden brown, pulls away from the sides of the pan, and springs back when lightly pressed, 35 to 40 minutes.

7. Invert the cake in the pan to cool to room temperature. If the pan doesn't have feet that lift the rim off the counter, invert the pan over a wine bottle (or something similar), inserting the neck of the bottle into the pan's center tube to suspend the pan above the counter.

continued . . .

continued from page 303

8. Run a thin knife blade around the cake to loosen the sides. Run the blade around the bottom of the cake to loosen and then release it onto a plate.

9. To make the compote: In a small saucepan, heat the preserves over low heat, stirring until melted. Stir in the lemon juice. Fold in the berries. Serve warm or at room temperature.

10. To serve, cut the cake into serving pieces with a serrated knife and top with the compote and whipped cream.

11. Cover leftover cake and store at room temperature for up to 2 days. Store the compote in a covered container in the refrigerator for up to 3 days. Reheat over low heat.

Makes 12 to 16 servings

TIP: *You'll need a 10-inch angel food pan, which is an aluminum tube pan with a removable bottom. Don't grease the pan. The light texture of angel food cake depends in part on the batter climbing the ungreased sides during baking and the cake cooling upside down.*

CHOCOLATE CHIP COOKIES

My dad has an intense sweet tooth, just like me. One afternoon when I was around ten years old, Dad got a hankering and he enlisted me to help him make Toll House chocolate chip cookies. That was the first time he and I had ever baked together. Since then, whenever I make chocolate chip cookies, including the ones from this recipe, I think of him and that special afternoon we spent together in the kitchen. I developed this recipe over the years, after experimenting with a few classics and having them come out flat every time. I wanted something that was chunky, beautiful, and also delicious. In the end, one big change I made was to cut back on the butter. I do truly believe that butter makes everything better and no one is more surprised than I am about how amazing these taste even though they're made with less of the good stuff than most traditional chocolate chip cookies.

PREP: *15 minutes*	**COOK**: *under 30 minutes*	**COOL**: *1 hour*

2½ cups all-purpose flour

1 heaping teaspoon baking soda

½ teaspoon sea salt

8 tablespoons (1 stick) unsalted butter, at room temperature

2 cups packed light brown sugar

2 large eggs

1½ teaspoons pure vanilla extract

1½ cups semisweet chocolate chips (see Tip)

1. Position a rack in the center of the oven and preheat the oven to 350°F. Line a baking sheet with parchment paper.

2. In a medium bowl, whisk together the flour, baking soda, and salt. Set aside.

3. In a stand mixer fitted with the paddle attachment (or in a large bowl with a handheld electric mixer), beat the butter and sugar on medium-high speed until light and fluffy, 2 to 3 minutes. Add the eggs and beat until blended. Add the vanilla and beat until blended.

4. Turn the mixer off and add the flour mixture to the bowl. Mix on medium just until the flour is mixed in, then turn the mixer to high speed for a few seconds to pull the dough together; it will be chunky.

5. Add the chocolate chips and beat on high for about 5 seconds to thoroughly and quickly mix in the chips.

6. Drop by large spoonfuls on the lined baking sheet; don't flatten them. Bake until lightly browned on top, 10 to 11 minutes. Cool on the pan on a rack for 1 minute, then transfer the cookies to the rack to cool completely. Repeat with the remaining dough.

7. Store the cookies in a tightly covered container at room temperature for up to 3 days.

Makes about 40 cookies

TIP: *Depending on what you're in the mood for, you can add ½ cup more or less chocolate than what is called for.*

MINA'S LEMON BARS

Whenever our good friend Gail brought us dinner during very busy periods of filming our show, she always included these bars for dessert, which she made from her mother's recipe. The kids love them, and they'd disappear pretty much the second we put them on the plate. Gail's mother, Mina, said that we could share the recipe here. I find that these bars are much easier to cut when they're completely cool.

PREP: *15 minutes*	**COOK**: *50 minutes*	**COOL**: *1 hour*

Nonstick baking spray or softened butter, for the pan

2 cups all-purpose flour

½ pound (2 sticks) salted butter, melted

½ cup powdered sugar, plus more for garnish

¼ teaspoon sea salt

2 cups granulated sugar

4 eggs, slightly beaten

5 tablespoons fresh lemon juice (from about 2 lemons)

1. Position a baking rack in the middle of the oven and preheat the oven to 350°F. Spray a 9 x 13-inch glass (see Tip) baking dish with baking spray or grease with butter.

2. In a medium bowl, combine the flour, melted butter, powdered sugar, and salt. Use a fork to stir gently until just barely combined; mixing as little as possible will result in a flakier crust. Use your fingers to press the mixture into the prepared pan.

3. Bake until the edges of the crust are very lightly browned, about 20 minutes.

4. Meanwhile, in a medium bowl, whisk together the granulated sugar, eggs, and lemon juice until well blended.

5. When the crust is done, pour the lemon mixture over the hot crust, return to the oven, and bake for 15 minutes. Gently tent a piece of foil on top to prevent overbrowning and bake until the top is lightly browned and the center is set when the pan is gently nudged, about 15 minutes.

6. Remove from the oven and dust the top with powdered sugar. Let cool completely on a rack in the pan, then cut into 15 bars or 30 squares. The bars are much easier to cut when completely cool.

7. Store in an airtight container at room temperature for up to 1 week. For longer storage, wrap in plastic or in zip-top bags and freeze for up to 1 month.

Makes 15 squares or 30 bite-size bars

TIP: *Only make these bars in a dish made from glass or other nonreactive material. Don't use an aluminum or other metal pan because the lemon will react to it.*

CHOCOLATE-DIPPED
SHORTBREAD COOKIES

*Sometimes simplicity is its own reward—and these buttery, vanilla-flavored
cookies dipped in chocolate are proof of that.*

PREP: *30 minutes, plus 30 minutes chilling*	COOK: *about 20 minutes*	COOL: *30 minutes, plus 1 hour setting*

COOKIES

3 cups all-purpose flour

1 cup sugar

¼ teaspoon kosher salt

¾ pound (3 sticks) salted butter, cut into pieces,
   at room temperature

4 teaspoons pure vanilla extract

GLAZE

12 ounces semisweet chocolate chips

2 teaspoons vegetable shortening

1. Line two baking sheets with parchment paper.

2. To make the cookies: In a food processor, pulse the flour, sugar, and salt to blend. Scatter the butter over the flour mixture. Add the vanilla. Pulse to form small clumps of dough.

3. Pour onto a work surface. Gently gather into a clump of cohesive dough. Divide in half. Form each piece into a log that is about 10 inches long and 2½ inches in diameter. Use a sharp knife to cut each log crosswise at ¾-inch intervals to form about 12 cookies each. Rotate the logs a quarter-turn between cuts to keep the logs round.

4. Transfer the cookies to the prepared baking sheets, spacing them at least 2 inches apart.

5. Cover lightly with plastic wrap and refrigerate until firm, about 30 minutes.

6. Position racks in the top third and middle of the oven and preheat the oven to 325°F.

7. Bake until the cookies are firm and pale golden on the edges, 18 to 20 minutes, switching racks and rotating the pans halfway through baking so that they bake evenly. Cool on the pan on a wire rack for 5 minutes, then transfer to wire racks to cool to room temperature.

8. To make the glaze: In a medium microwave-safe bowl, combine the chocolate chips and shortening. Melt in the microwave in 20-second increments on 50% power, stirring after each increment, until the chips begin to lose their shape. Stir until melted and smooth.

9. Dip one half of each cookie into the melted chocolate, let excess drip off, and place on a wire rack. Let stand until the chocolate is set, about 1 hour.

10. Store in an airtight container at room temperature for up to 4 days.

Makes about 2 dozen cookies

LEMON & LAVENDER ICEBOX COOKIES

Lemon and lavender go together so well, and these simple cookies perfectly show off this delicious combination. "Icebox" cookies are a busy person's best friend. Every now and then—usually when I'm preparing other things to serve right away and I already have the food processor out—I'll spend a few minutes mixing up the dough and freeze the log. Then, whenever I want to quickly prepare a batch of cookies for the kids or friends stopping by, all I have to do is slice and bake. For a fun twist, try the Key lime variation on the next page. Key limes are sharper and more acidic than regular Persian limes. I make the cookies with fresh juice when Key limes are in season, and with bottled Key lime juice the rest of the year.

PREP: *20 minutes, plus at least 4 hours chilling*	COOK: *under 15 minutes*	COOL: *1 hour*

2 cups all-purpose flour

1 cup powdered sugar

½ cup cornstarch

¾ teaspoon kosher salt

4 teaspoons lightly packed grated lemon zest

1 teaspoon food-grade dried lavender or 2 teaspoons fresh

½ pound (2 sticks) salted butter, cut into pats and chilled

2 large egg yolks

½ teaspoon pure vanilla extract

½ teaspoon lemon extract

1. In a food processor, pulse together the flour, powdered sugar, cornstarch, salt, lemon zest, and lavender until well blended. Scatter the butter over the flour mixture and pulse until the mixture resembles wet sand.

2. In a small bowl, whisk together the egg yolks and extracts. Drizzle over the flour mixture and pulse only until large clumps of dough form.

3. Pour the dough onto a work surface and cut in half. Form each piece into a log that is 8 inches long and about 2 inches in diameter. Wrap each log in plastic wrap and twist the ends closed to smooth the surface of the logs. Refrigerate until deeply chilled, at least 4 hours and preferably overnight. (The logs can be wrapped in foil at this point and frozen for up to 1 month. Let stand on the counter for about 20 minutes or until slightly softened before continuing.)

4. Position racks in the top and bottom third of the oven and preheat the oven to 350°F. Line two baking sheets with parchment paper.

5. Using a sharp knife, cut each log into 18 rounds, each a scant ½ inch thick. Rotate the logs a quarter-turn between cuts to keep the logs round. Arrange the cookies at least 1 inch apart on the prepared baking sheets.

continued . . .

continued from page 313

6. Bake until firm and golden on the edges, 10 to 12 minutes, switching racks and rotating the pans halfway through baking so that they bake evenly. Cool on the pans on wire racks for 5 minutes, then transfer to the racks with a firm spatula to cool to room temperature.

7. Store the cookies in an airtight container at room temperature for up to 3 days.

Makes 3 dozen

KEY LIME ICEBOX COOKIES

Follow the directions for Lemon and Lavender Icebox Cookies, using an equal amount of grated lime zest in place of the lemon zest. Omit the lavender.

Increase the vanilla extract to 1 teaspoon and use 2 tablespoons bottled or fresh Key lime juice in place of the lemon extract.

If desired, while the cookies are still warm yet firm enough to handle, gently and evenly coat them one at a time in ¾ cup powdered sugar for a festive look. Place on a wire rack to cool to room temperature before serving.

LEMON POPPY SEED BREAD

Not only is this dessert easy to make, it's also a perfect pick-me-up after school or for breakfast with a big mug of hot coffee.

PREP: *15 minutes*	**COOK**: *about 1 hour*	**COOL**: *1 hour*

LEMON POPPY SEED BREAD
Vegetable oil spray
2½ cups all-purpose flour
1 tablespoon poppy seeds
1 tablespoon baking powder
½ teaspoon baking soda
¾ teaspoon kosher salt
1⅔ cups sugar
⅔ cup milk
½ cup vegetable oil

3 large eggs
2 teaspoons grated lemon zest
2 tablespoons fresh lemon juice
1 teaspoon pure vanilla extract

LEMON DRIZZLE
1½ cups powdered sugar
1 tablespoon grated lemon zest
2 tablespoons fresh lemon juice, or as needed

1. To make the lemon poppy seed bread: Preheat the oven to 350°F. Generously spray a 9 x 5-inch loaf pan with vegetable oil, making sure to cover the bottom and sides very well.

2. In a medium bowl, whisk together the flour, poppy seeds, baking powder, baking soda, and salt.

3. In a large bowl, combine the sugar, milk, oil, eggs, lemon zest, lemon juice, and vanilla and whisk until well blended. Add the dry ingredients to the liquid and stir just until combined. Don't overmix.

4. Scrape the batter into the prepared pan. Bake until a tester inserted in the center comes out clean, about 1 hour. Let cool in the pan on a rack for 10 to 15 minutes, then unmold onto the rack to cool completely.

5. To make the lemon drizzle: Sift the powdered sugar into a medium bowl. Add the lemon zest and stir to distribute it. Stir in 1 tablespoon water and as much of the lemon juice as is necessary to make a pourable icing.

6. Pour the drizzle over the warm or room-temperature bread.

7. Tightly wrap and store at room temperature for up to 3 days.

Makes 8 servings

ACKNOWLEDGMENTS

First and foremost, thank you to Chip, my biggest fan and my most willing taste tester. To our children, whose love language is food, thank you for teaching me how special it is to share a meal around the table. To my mom, Bevie, and Gail Holt, for sharing your recipes that have become some of our family's favorites. A big thank-you to the entire team at William Morrow/HarperCollins—Cassie Jones, Kara Zauberman, Liate Stehlik, Lynn Grady, Tavia Kowalchuk, Anwesha Basu, Nyamekye Waliyaya, Rachel Meyers, Suet Chong, Anna Brower, and Kate Slate—without whom there would be no finished book in your hands. And to Mark Chamlin, Bill Stankey, and David Vigliano for helping us get this project off the ground.

To my home team at Magnolia—Emily Paben, Alissa Neely, Whitney Kauffold, Kelsie Monsen, Billy Jack Brawner, Kaila Luna, Beth Chiles, Hannah Midgett, Kayli Nuce, and Stephen Lewis—for believing in my vision for this book and helping bring it to life.

To the photographers and stylists, Amy Neunsinger, Frances Boswell, and Kate Martindale. And to Andre Junget for such stunning illustrations. Thank you all for making these pages infinitely more beautiful.

To the fearless recipe team leader, Becki Shepherd, who I'm so thankful to have meal swapped with for so many years, thank you for sharing your gift with my family and our team at Magnolia Table. And to Sheri Castle, Jamie Flanagan, and Nicole McDuffie, who combed through, cooked, and tasted each recipe carefully to make sure we've shared all the information you may need.

To Marah Stets, for your patience and help getting all of my recipes, thoughts, and ideas on paper. And for never judging me for using too much butter!

And a heartfelt thank-you to all of my family and friends. It for sure takes a village, and I'm so thankful for everyone who helped me get this book across the finish line.

UNIVERSAL CONVERSION CHART

OVEN TEMPERATURE EQUIVALENTS

250°F = 120°C

275°F = 135°C

300°F = 150°C

325°F = 160°C

350°F = 180°C

375°F = 190°C

400°F = 200°C

425°F = 220°C

450°F = 230°C

475°F = 240°C

500°F = 260°C

MEASUREMENT EQUIVALENTS

Measurements should always be level unless directed otherwise.

⅛ teaspoon = 0.5 mL

¼ teaspoon = 1 mL

½ teaspoon = 2 mL

1 teaspoon = 5 mL

1 tablespoon = 3 teaspoons = ½ fluid ounce = 15 mL

2 tablespoons = ⅛ cup = 1 fluid ounce = 30 mL

4 tablespoons = ¼ cup = 2 fluid ounces = 60 mL

5⅓ tablespoons = ⅓ cup = 3 fluid ounces = 80 mL

8 tablespoons = ½ cup = 4 fluid ounces = 120 mL

10⅔ tablespoons = ⅔ cup = 5 fluid ounces = 160 mL

12 tablespoons = ¾ cup = 6 fluid ounces = 180 mL

16 tablespoons = 1 cup = 8 fluid ounces = 240 mL

INDEX

Note: Page references in *italics* indicate photographs.